AF650040

Viva *Catch*Up

BIOLOGY

Viva CatchUp

BIOLOGY

For Class X

Madhur Gupta

Viva Books

New Delhi | Mumbai | Chennai | Kolkata | Bangalore | Hyderabad | Kochi | Guwahati

First Published 2009

Viva Books Private Limited

4737/23, Ansari Road, Daryaganj, New Delhi 110 002
Tel. 42242200, 23258325, 23283121, Email: vivadelhi@vivagroupindia.net

76, Service Industries, Shirvane, Sector 1, Nerul, Navi Mumbai 400 706
Tel. 27721273, 27721274, Email: vivamumbai@vivagroupindia.net

Jamals Fazal Chambers, 26 Greams Road, Chennai 600 006
Tel. 28294241, 28290304, Email: vivachennai@vivagroupindia.net

B-103, Jindal Towers, 21/1A/3 Darga Road, Kolkata 700 017
Tel. 22816713, Email: vivakolkata@vivagroupindia.net

7, GF, Sovereign Park Aptts., 56-58, K. R. Road, Basavanagudi, Bangalore 560 004
Tel. 26607409, Email: vivabangalore@vivagroupindia.net

101-102, Moghal Marc Apartments, 3-4-637 to 641, Narayanguda,
Hyderabad 500 029, Tel. 27564481, Email: vivahyderabad@vivagroupindia.net

First Floor, Beevi Towers, SRM Road, Kaloor, Kochi - 682 018, Kerala,
Tel. 0484-2403055, 2403056, Email: vivakochi@vivagroupindia.net

232, GNB Road, Beside UCO Bank, Silpukhuri, Guwahati 781 003
Tel. 0361-2666386, Email: vivaguwahati@vivagroupindia.net

www.vivagroupindia.com

ISBN: 978-81-309-0840-3

Published by Vinod Vasishtha for Viva Books Private Limited
4737/23 Ansari Road, Daryaganj, New Delhi 110 002

Printed & bound by Narain Printers, Noida 201 301

CONTENTS

PREFACE

The book *Viva CatchUp Biology* is written in accordance with the latest syllabus prescribed by CBSE for class X for science subject.

This book is not intended to replace school textbooks. As tests and examinations approach, however, many students feel the need to revise from something a good deal shorter than their usual textbook. This book is intended to fill that need.

The text has been written in a simple and easy-to-understand style. The concepts have been explained in point-wise formats that also aids quick learning. The diagrams given are fairly-large in size, they have been appropriately coloured, drawn and labelled as clearly as possible.

The book has been written in the hope that apart from preparing themselves for board examinations, students will also recognize and understand some of the basic principles of biology. There are exercises given at the end of each chapter. The questions in the exercises have been divided into four groups as per the examination pattern. A set of Test Yourself questions along with the answers gives an idea as to how well the topic has been grasped.

I thank Ms Bhavna Saxena of Viva Books for her suggestions and active involvement in the project.

I welcome all kinds of feedback from teachers and students to further improve the book in the next edition.

Madhur Gupta

1 NUTRITION

Life processes

- Living organisms are well organised structures, consisting in most cases of organ systems, organs, tissues and cells.
  - The processes important for the maintenance of living organisms are called **life processes**. The following life processes are required for maintenance of life:

Nutrition	Getting food
Respiration	Releasing energy from food
Transportation	Moving substances from one place to another within the body
Excretion	Getting rid of waste from the body

  - In single-celled organisms, the different life processes take place through the entire surface of the organisms by the process of **diffusion**. However, in multicellular organisms, because of big body size and complex body designs, simple process of diffusion is not sufficient to meet the requirements of performing different functions. Different life processes with specialized body parts have, therefore, developed.

Nutrition and its types

- All living organisms need food to live and grow. The cell is the basic unit of all organisms.
- **Nutrition** is the process of intake of food, digesting it and utilizing it for the growth and maintenance of the body.

Did you know that energy is used even when we are asleep? This is because the cells in our body are continuously working. The heart beats without a break. We breathe in and breathe out even while sleeping.

☞ **Remember the sequence:**

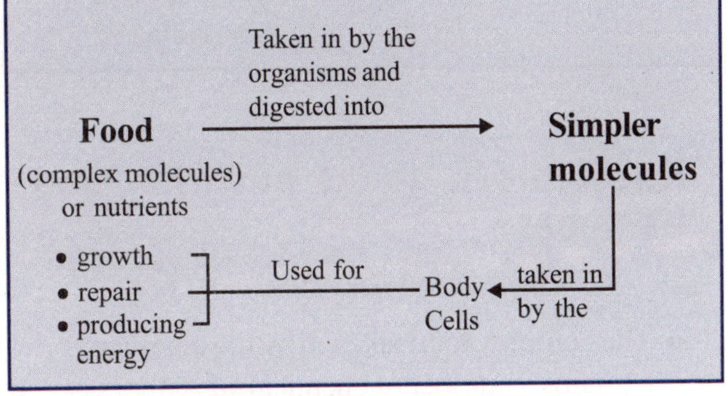

- There are two main types of nutrition: **autotrophic** and **heterotrophic**.
  - 'Autotroph' term has a Greek origin where 'auto' means self and 'troph' refers to

nutrition. In autotrophic nutrition, an organism makes its own food from simple raw materials (inorganic substances). Green plants and autotrophic bacteria prepare their food (organic material) from carbon dioxide, minerals and water (inorganic substances) in the presence of sunlight by the process of **photosynthesis**.

- In Greek 'hetero' means other. Hence in heterotrophic nutrition, organisms obtain food (in the form of organic substances) from other organisms and then digest it into simpler forms for utilisation with the help of **enzymes**, also called as biocatalysts. Heterotrophic organisms or heterotrophs are divided into parasitic, saprophytic and holozoic forms depending upon the mode of intake of food.

  Enzymes are organic catalysts which speed up chemical reactions within cells or organisms.

☞ **Remember the types:**

- Nutrition
  - Autotrophic
  - Heterotrophic
    - Parasitic
    - Saprophytic
    - Holozoic

Know more about nutrition and its types

- The complex food taken in by the organism contains a number of chemical substances called **nutrients**.
- The nutrients in food are **carbohydrates, fats, proteins, vitamins** and **minerals**.
- The site of food production in green plants is the **chloroplast** which contains **chlorophyll** pigment. This pigment is capable of trapping and fixing the solar energy.
- **Holozoic** organisms ingest complex food, which is then digested by the enzymes released inside the body.
- **Digestion** is the process of converting complex food substances into simpler molecules which can be absorbed by the cells.
- The undigested food is **egested** (removal from the body).
- Holozoic nutrition is found in almost all animals. For example, *Amoeba,* frog and man.
- Some organisms derive nutrition from other organisms without killing them. This type of nutrition is called **parasitic**. Examples of parasitic animals are tapeworms, leeches, lice, ticks and malarial parasite; parasitic plants are amarbel **(cuscuta)**, some fungi and bacteria.
- In saprophytic mode, organisms feed on dead and decaying organic matter. Examples are fungi (like yeast, bread mould, mushrooms) and many bacteria.

Questions

1. Why is digestion needed? (1 mark)
2. What are enzymes? (1 mark)

Autotrophic nutrition

Like other organisms, plants also need energy and nourishment to maintain life functions. They make their own food (organic nutrients) by the process of photosynthesis.

Photosynthesis

- Photosynthesis is a chemical process that traps the energy of sunlight.

- Plant cells use the energy to convert carbon dioxide and water into sugars (carbohydrates). The chemical reaction involved in the process is:

$$\underset{\text{(from air)}}{6CO_2} + \underset{\text{(from soil)}}{6H_2O} \xrightarrow[\text{sunlight}]{\text{chlorophyll (present in leaves)}} \underset{\text{Sugar}}{C_6H_{12}O_6} + 6O_2$$

- There are a number of chemical reactions that take place in the process of photosynthesis. You will study about these reactions in your higher classes. The reactions happen inside chloroplasts. Chloroplasts are the organelles present in the cells of leaves and other green parts of plants.
- Leaf is the major site of photosynthesis. The process of photosynthesis can be divided into three steps:
  (a) Absorption of light energy by chlorophyll.
  (b) Conversion of light energy to chemical energy and splitting of water molecules, in the presence of light into hydrogen and oxygen.
  (c) Reduction of carbon dioxide to carbohydrates.
- The first two steps require light and are a part of **light reaction**.

  The third step does not require light and is called the **dark reaction**.
- The excess sugar or carbohydrates which are not utilized immediately are stored in the form of **starch** which acts as the internal energy reserve.

The numbers on the concept map on pages 4–5 refer to the checklist of points below.

Checklist for photosynthesis

1 ◆ Leaves are so arranged that the lower ones are not overshadowed by those above and most of the leaves are exposed to direct sunlight.

◆ The leaf blade is flat and thin, so that a large surface area is exposed for the absorption of light and even the lower layers of cells receive light.

2 ◆ Roots absorb water and minerals from the soil by the process of osmosis (osmosis is the process by which a liquid moves gradually from one cell to another through a semipermeable membrane due to concentration gradient). Water and minerals move up to leaves through xylem in the **transpiration stream**.

◆ Minerals are needed not only for photosynthesis but also for general development of plants. Nitrogen, phosphorus, iron and magnesium are the important minerals taken up from the soil. Nitrogen is essential for the synthesis of proteins and other compounds. It is absorbed both as inorganic (nitrates or nitrites) and organic compounds. Certain bacteria convert the atmospheric nitrogen to nitrogenous compounds which are absorbed by plants through water from the soil.

◆ **Carbon dioxide** present in the atmosphere enters leaves through stomata. The aquatic plants utilise carbon dioxide dissolved in water. The desert plants take up carbon dioxide at night and convert it into an intermediate which is then stored. This intermediate is acted upon by light, during the day, and reduced to carbohydrates.

3 ◆ All green parts of the plant have chlorophyll. It is a pigment present in the cell organelles called chloroplasts. Chloroplasts are visible as green dots in a cross-section of a leaf under a microscope.

◆ There are air spaces in the leaf cells.

◆ The spaces allow carbon dioxide and water vapour to circulate freely within the leaf, bringing the raw materials for photosynthesis to the leaf cells.

4 ◆ Tiny pores are present on the surface of the leaves. These pores actually consists of a **stomatal pore** which is surrounded by two kidney-shaped **guard cells**.

◆ Gaseous exchange occurs through these stomatal pores.

Getting sunlight

Getting the raw materials

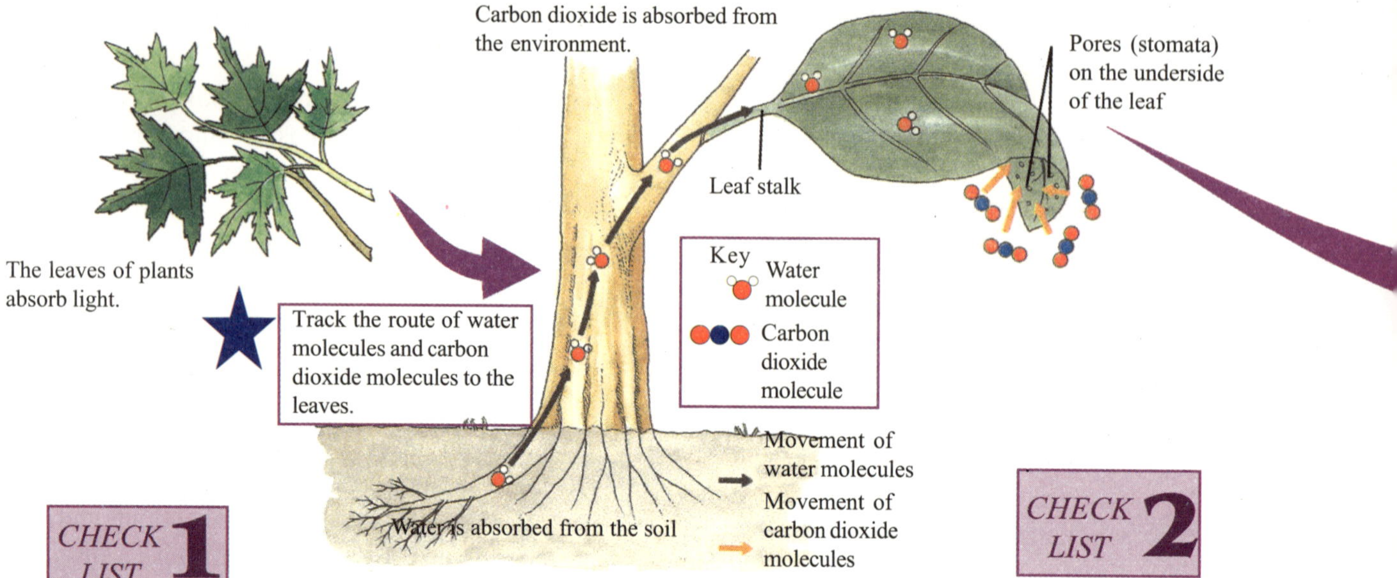

CHECK LIST 1

CHECK LIST 2

Mechanism of photosynthesis

CHECK LIST 5

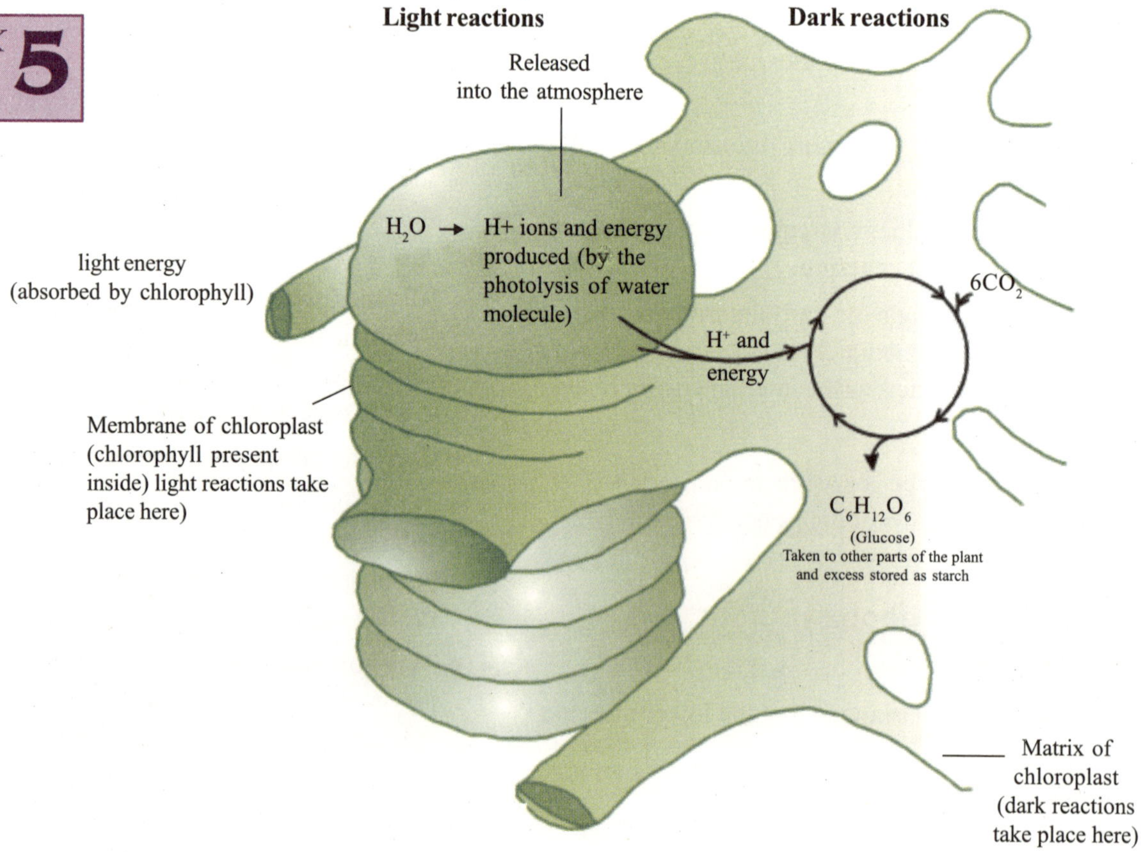

Track the route of water molecules and carbon dioxide molecules inside the leaves.

Inside the leaf

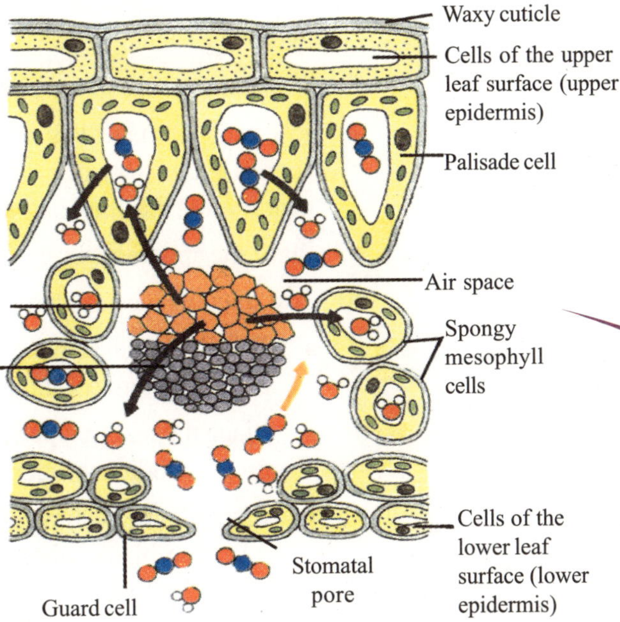

Track the route of water molecules and carbon dioxide molecules to the chloroplasts.

CHECK LIST 3

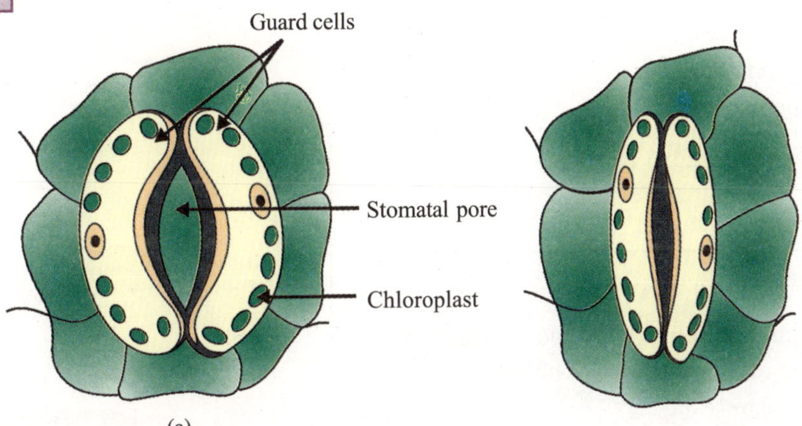

(a) (b)

CHECK LIST 4

- If stomata remain open, large amount of water can also be lost through them; thus, plants close these pores when carbon dioxide is not required for photosynthesis.

  Movement of guard cells controls the opening and closing of stomata. The guard cells swell when water flows into them causing the stomatal pore to open. Similarly the pore closes if the guard cells shrink.
- The exchange of gases occurs across the surface of stem, roots and leaves as well.

5 ◆ **Mechanism of Photosynthesis**

- Chlorophyll present inside chloroplasts absorbs light energy.
- This energy brings about the breakdown of water molecule into H^+ ions and energy.

  The oxygen molecules are released into the atmosphere.

$$H_2O \rightarrow H^+ + OH^- + \text{energy}$$

- Hydrogen ions are used to reduce CO_2 molecule to carbohydrates.

$$CO_2 \xrightarrow{H^+} C_6H_{12}O_6$$

Remember

- * Chlorophyll present in the chloroplast is the main site of light reaction of photosynthesis in green plants.
- * Oxygen released during photosynthesis comes from water and not carbon dioxide.

Activity 1

To show the need for carbon dioxide in photosynthesis.

1. Select a potted plant with long leaves and place it in the dark for 48 hours in order to destarch the leaves.
2. Take a wide-mouthed bottle with potassium hydroxide solution in it.
3. Cover the mouth of the bottle with a split cork.
4. Insert one of the leaves in the bottle through the cork in such a way that half of the leaf remains inside while the other half remains outside.
5. Place the apparatus in sunlight for 3 to 4 hours.
6. Test the presence of starch in the leaf.
   - Boil the leaf in alcohol, to remove chlorophyll and it will turn colourless.
   - Place the leaf in a petri dish and add a few drops of iodine solution.
   - Part of leaf which was outside the bottle will turn blue-black, whereas the part of the leaf inside the bottle will not turn blue-black. This shows that the part of leaf (inside the bottle)

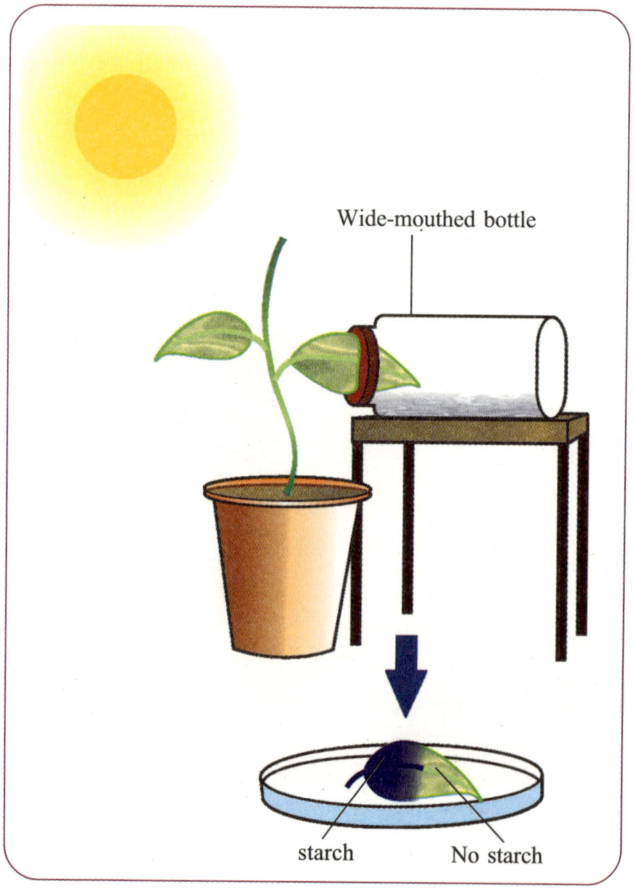

Carbon dioxide is necessary for photosynthesis

which did not get carbon dioxide (it was absorbed by potassium hydroxide solution) could not produce starch.

7. **Conclusion:** Photosynthesis does not occur in the part of leaf inside the bottle which is devoid of CO_2. Hence, carbon dioxide is necessary for photosynthesis.

Activity 2

To show the need for chlorophyll in photosynthesis.

1. Take a potted plant with variegated leaves (such leaves contain both green and white or yellow parts in the same leaf) and keep it in the dark for 48 hours to destarch the leaves.

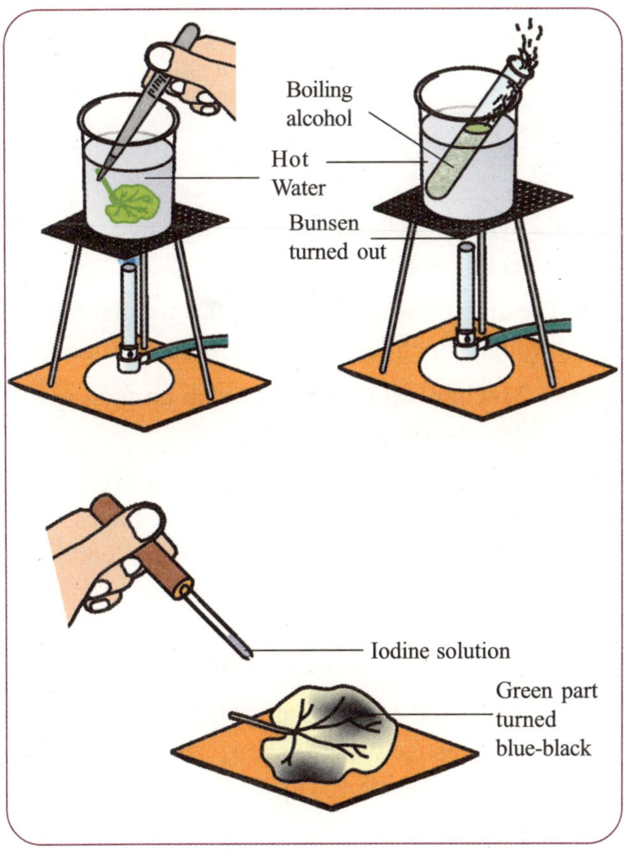

Chlorophyll is necessary for photosynthesis

2. Now keep this plant in the sunlight for a few hours and pluck a few leaves.
3. Boil these leaves in water for a few minutes to denature the enzyme and subsequently in alcohol.
   - The leaves will turn colourless due to loss of chlorophyll.
4. To test for the presence of starch, add a few drops of iodine solution on the leaves after washing them with water.
   - The portion of the leaf that was green earlier will turn blue-black, whereas the non-green part will not turn blue-black.
5. **Conclusion:** Starch is produced only in the green region. Hence, chlorophyll is necessary for photosynthesis.

Questions

1. Define photosynthesis. (1 mark)
2. Write the overall reaction of photosynthesis. (1 mark)
3. How will you show the presence of starch in a leaf? (3 marks)

Heterotrophic nutrition

Heterotrophic nutrition is seen in case of the consumers, i.e., animals and fungi.

The mode of nutrition, food intake, digestive organs and the process of digestion are different for different animals. For example, a deer eats grass which is stationary. On the other hand, a lion eats deer which is mobile. Both deer and the lion will have different strategies to procure their food. They will show different digestive systems as the one is a herbivore and the other is a carnivore.

Steps in nutrition

Different steps are shown in the following flow chart.

Ingestion
food is taken into the mouth

↓

Digestion
large insoluble molecules of food are broken down into smaller soluble molecules

↓

Absorption
the small molecules of digested food pass into the body

→ **Assimilation** follows the absorption of digested food. It includes the processes in cells that convert absorbed food materials into living matter.

↓

Egestion
undigested food is removed from the body through the anus

Nutrition in Human beings

- The different steps of nutrition take place in the **digestive system**.
- The digestive system consists of **alimentary canal** and the **associated digestive glands**.
- The **alimentary canal** is a nearly nine-metre long muscular tube, running through the body. It extends from the mouth to the anus.

The alimentary canal consists of the following parts or organs:

The **mouth** and buccal cavity, pharynx (throat), oesophagus (gullet), stomach, small intestine (duodenum, jejunum and ileum), large intestine (caecum, colon and rectum) and anus.

The **buccal cavity** is the cavity where the mouth opens. It is the space containing the tongue and teeth.

The **oesophagus** is a straight, narrow, thick-walled muscular tube, leading from the **pharynx** to the stomach. **Peristaltic movement**, i.e., contraction of muscular walls of oesophagus makes the food move through it.

From **stomach** exit of food is regulated by a sphincter muscle which releases it in small amounts into small intestine.

The **intestine** is a long tube through which food travels from the stomach and out of the body while it is being digested.

The **digestive glands** associated with the digestive system are the salivary glands, liver and pancreas. They pour their secretions into the alimentary canal through tubes **(ducts)**. Some of the digestive enzymes are produced by cells in the wall of the alimentary canal.

Digesting Food

- Food is processed through the digestive system in the following sequence:
- The digestive system includes a muscular tube through which food moves. It processes food.
    - **Mechanical processes** break up food and mix it with digestive juices.
    - **Chemical processes** digest food using different enzymes in the digestive juices. The body cannot absorb the large insoluble molecules of carbohydrate, protein and fat in food. They are broken down into smaller soluble molecules which the body can absorb.
- The liver and pancreas are connected by ducts to the digestive system. They play an important role in the digestion of food.

The numbers on the concept map on page 10 refer to the checklist below.

Checklist for the digestive system

(M) = mechanical processes of digestion

(C) = chemical processes of digestion

1 ◆ **(M)Teeth** chew food, breaking it into small pieces.

The surface area of food exposed to the action of digestive enzymes is increased.

2 ◆ **(C) Saliva,** produced by the salivary glands, contains the enzyme ptyalin (salivary amylase) which digests starch into maltose. Thus, the digestion of starch begins in the mouth.

◆ **(M)** Saliva moistens the food and makes it slippery for easy swallowing.

3 ◆ **(M)** Muscles of the **stomach** wall and small **intestine** mix food thoroughly with different juices containing digestive enzymes.

As a result, food and digestive enzymes are brought into intimate contact and a liquid paste called **chyme** is formed.

◆ **(C)** Gastric juice, produced by **pits** in the stomach wall, contains **hydrochloric acid** and the enzymes **pepsin** and **renin** and a small amount of gastric **lipase**.

- **Hydrochloric acid** increases the acidity of the stomach contents.

  As a result, bacteria in the food are killed and the action of salivary amylase is stopped.

  Also the protein-digesting enzyme, pepsin acts in acidic medium. The stomach wall lining is not affected by acid due to secretion of mucus along with the gastric juice.

- **Pepsin** breaks down proteins into peptones.
- **Renin** clots milk, making it semi-solid.

  As a result, milk stays in the gut long enough to be digested.

- **Gastric lipase** partially breaks down lipids.

4 ◆ **(C) Bile**, produced by the **liver**, is a green alkaline liquid which is stored in the gall bladder before release into the small intestine through the bile duct. It

- neutralises acid from the stomach, and
- breaks fats and oils into small droplets (**emulsification**).

As a result, the surface area of fats and oils exposed to the action of the enzyme **lipase** is increased.

As a result, fats and oils are digested more quickly.

5 ◆ **(C) Pancreatic juice**, produced by the **pancreas**, is released into the small intestine through the pancreatic duct. It contains:

- **bicarbonate ions secreted by duodenal wall** neutralise stomach acid and make the medium alkaline for the action of pancreatic enzymes.
- **pancreatic amylase, trypsin** and **lipases** which digest starch proteins, fats and oils.

◆ The digestive enzymes are secreted by **exocrine** region of pancreas. On the other hand, the endocrine region secretes hormones **insulin** and **glucagon**.

6 ◆ **(C) Intestinal juice**, produced by glands in the wall of the **duodenum** and **ileum**, contains:

- **carbohydrases** and **lipases** that complete the digestion of carbohydrates, fats and oils.

◆ Once the digestion is complete, proteins are converted to amino acids, carbohydrates to glucose, and lipids into fatty acids and glycerol.

◆ **Dental caries** is an infectious disease that causes gradual softening of enamel and dentine. It is caused by certain types of acid-producing bacteria. The acid softens or demineralises the enamel and **dental plaque** is formed on the tooth. This does not allow the saliva to reach the tooth surface to neutralise acid. With regular brushing of the teeth, plaque can be removed and bacteria can be prevented from producing acids.

THE HUMAN DIGESTIVE SYSTEM

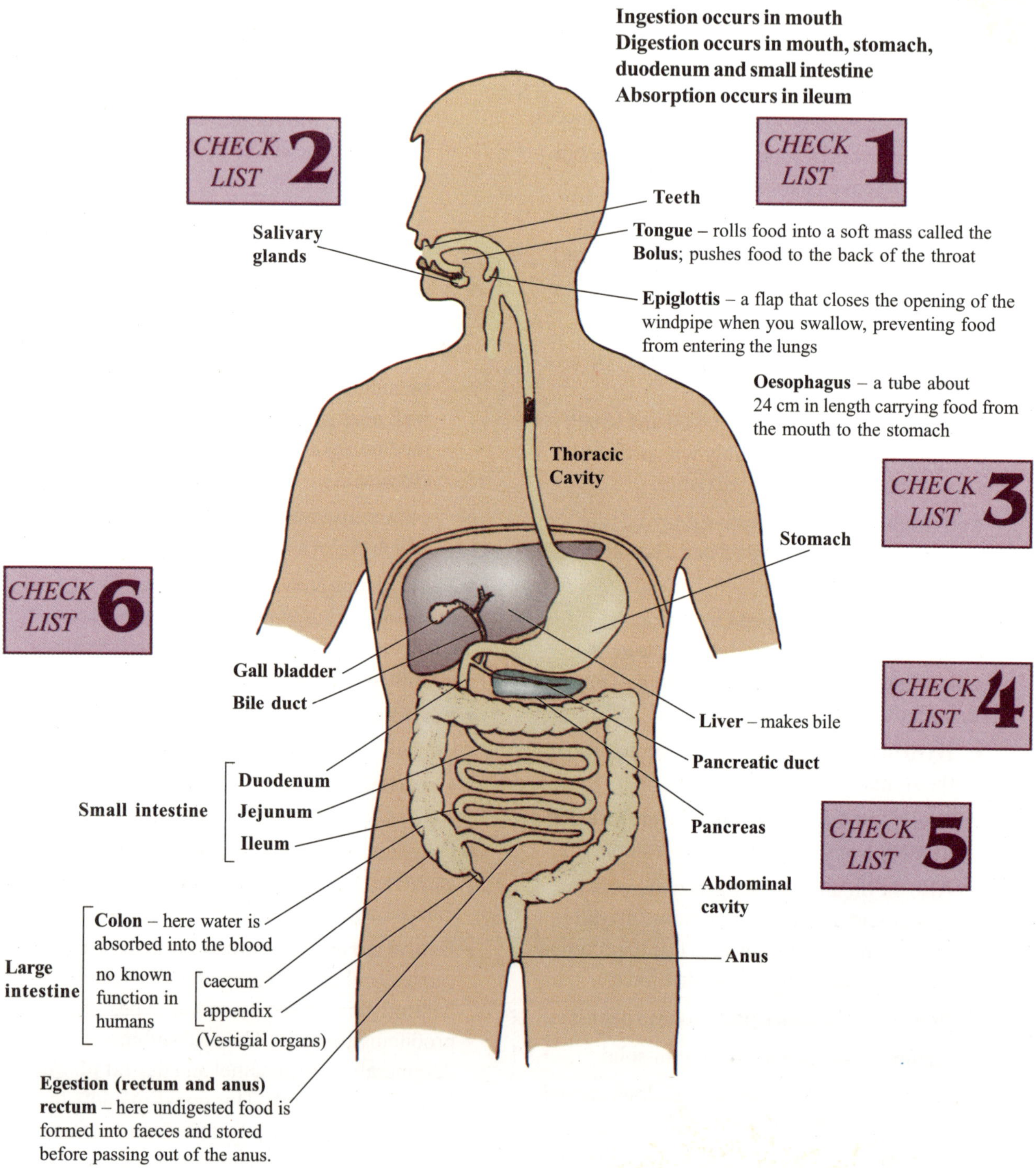

Chemistry of digestion

Digestive enzymes catalyse the breakdown of food by **hydrolysis**. Water splits large insoluble molecules of food into smaller soluble molecules which are suitable for absorption into the body.

Digested food is absorbed by the walls of small intestine which are provided with numerous long finger-like projections called **villi**. They increase the surface area for absorption of food.

The food which is not absorbed is passed on into the large intestine. Here too villi are present which absorb water from the remaining unabsorbed food eventually converting it to faeces. These are removed from the body via the anus. The exit is regulated by anal sphincter.

Questions

1. Name the final products of digestion. (2 marks)
2. In which part of the digestive system is (2 marks)
   (a) Protein digested
   (b) Starch digested.

☞ Remember

* Omnivores eat both plants and meat
* Herbivores eat plants
* Carnivores eat meat.

The length of small intestine is different depending on the food they eat. Herbivores have longer small intestine than the carnivores. This is because herbivores eat grass that contains cellulose which takes longer time to digest. On the other hand, carnivores need to digest meat.

Humans are omnivores and the human digestive system is adapted to deal with a mixture of plant and animal foods. The unicellular organism *Amoeba* is also omnivorous. It does not have a complex digestive system but it has digestive enzymes. Grasshopper is herbivorous and its digestive system is adapted to deal with plant leaves.

Nutrition in *Amoeba* and *Paramoecium*

Amoeba It feeds on microscopic, aquatic animals and plants. Nutrition in *Amoeba* is holozoic. It ingests its food by the process of **phagocytosis.** It throws out a number of small projections (called **pseudopodia**) from the body to engulf the food particle. The ingested food is enclosed in the newly formed **food vacuole** along with a few **lysosomes** (present in the cytoplasm). The enzymes present in lysosomes digest the food, which is then diffused in the cytoplasm (**assimilation**). The undigested food remains in the food vacuole and is thrown out of the body, by a process called egestion.

Paramoecium It is a unicellular organism with a definite shape. The food enters the cell at a specific spot. Cilia, which cover the entire surface of the cell, help in the movement of food towards the spot, through which it enters the cell.

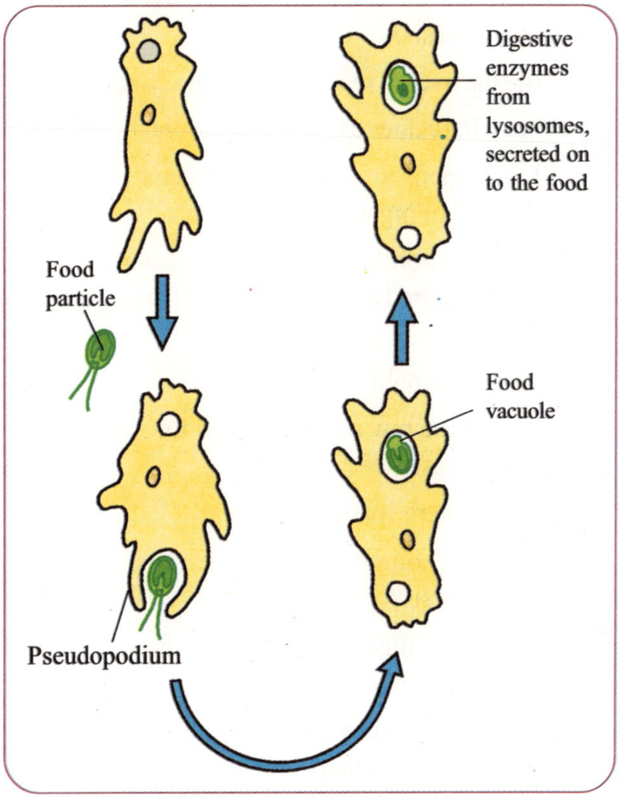

Nutrition in *Amoeba*

EXERCISES

I. Very Short Answer Questions

(1 mark)

1. What criteria do we use to decide whether something is alive?
2. Why is nutrition important for an organism?
3. What is the source of oxygen in photosynthesis?
4. Which cells of the leaf are mainly involved in photosynthesis?
5. Write the overall reaction for photosynthesis.
6. From where does carbon dioxide enters the leaf?
7. What happens to green leaves when they are dipped in boiling water and alcohol?
8. Which is the only natural process that gives out oxygen required for respiration of living organisms?
9. Define autotrophic nutrition.
10. What are the raw materials used for photosynthesis?
11. Why are there spaces in the leaf cells?
12. What is the source of energy used by plants in photosynthesis?
13. Name the vestigial organ found in the alimentary canal of humans.
14. How does food move from mouth to stomach in an alimentary canal?
15. Why is that the lining of stomach wall is not affected by the hydrochloric acid produced?
16. Name the gland in the human body which secretes both enzymes and hormones.
17. What is the role of liver in digestion?
18. How is the action of ptyalin ends in stomach?
19. What are the two important functions of the large intestine?
20. Define assimilation.
21. What do you mean by egestion?
22. Name the enzyme that initates the digestion of proteins in man.
23. How is the digested food passed on to the cells of the body?
24. Define the term emulsification.
25. Give an example of a parasitic animal.
26. Name the protein digesting enzyme present in gastric juice.
27. Which part of the alimentary canal in man absorbs water from the digested food?
28. What is the function of villi in the intestine of man?
29. Name the three parts of the small intestine.
30. Which ions make the medium alkaline in duodenum?
31. In which part of alimentary canal the salivary glands pour their secretions?

32. What is the role of gall bladder?
33. Why are the digestive enzymes called as hydrolases?
34. How cilia help *Paramoecium* in nutrition?
35. Name the acid produced by stomach in humans.
36. What is the role of bicarbonate ions secreted by duodenal walls of small intestine?
37. Explain the term dental caries.
38. Name the largest gland found in man.

II. Short Answer Questions

(2 marks)

1. How are saprophytes different from holozoic mode of nutrition?
2. Why do leaves appear green?
3. How does gall bladder, help in the digestion process?
4. State the role played by each in photosynthesis:
   a. Water b. Chlorophyll.
5. Name two plants with variegated leaves.
6. Discuss the role of food vacuoles in *Amoeba*.
7. How is small intestine adapted for the absorption of food?
8. How is the major nutrient present in *chapatis* digested and absorbed?
9. Where are salivary glands situated in a man? What are their functions?
10. Why chewing of food is important in the process of digestion?
11. How is ingestion different from egestion?
12. What is the role of tongue in the process of digestion?
13. Mention any two ways in which digested food is utilized by the body.
14. What is the role of hydrochloric acid secreted in the stomach of man?
15. List the functions of pancreas.
16. How are proteins digested in the alimentary canal?
17. Why is diffusion insufficient to meet the oxygen requirements of multicellular organisms like humans?
18. What are the differences between autotrophic and heterotrophic nutrition?
19. Why in case of water deficiency, is the rate of photosynthesis lowered?
20. Why is the small intestine of herbivores longer than that of carnivores?

III. Short Answer Questions

(3 marks)

1. What are the main features that make leaves suitable for photosynthesis?
2. 'All life on earth would come to an end if there were no green plants.' Comment.
3. What are the end products of digestion of carbohydrates, proteins and fats?
4. Write the function of each of the following in photosynthesis:
   (a) Water (b) Chlorophyll
   (c) Stomata.
5. 'Bile does not contain any digestive enzymes still it is essential for digestion.' Justify.
6. What is the role of following enzymes in digestion of food?
   (a) Amylase (b) Pepsin
   (c) Lipase
7. Distinguish between saprophytic and autotrophic mode of nutrition.

8. Differentiate between digestion and assimilation.
9. What is emulsification and how it is carried out during the process of digestion in man?
10. Write a short account of parasites. Give examples.
11. Differentiate between herbivores and carnivores.
12. Describe the largest gland present in the human body associated with the process of digestion. Mention its functions.
13. Explain the process of digestion that occurs in duodenum.
14. What is the function of digestive enzymes?
15. Name one enzyme each responsible for digestion of
    a. Sugar b. Protein c. Fats.
16. How does *Paramoecium* process its food?
17. Write a short note on dental caries.

IV. Long Answer Questions

(5 marks)

1. Mention the mode of nutrition and food habits of the following organisms.
    (a) Frog (b) Amoeba
    (c) Tapeworm (d) Mango tree
    (e) Bacteria
2. Briefly discuss the structure and function of stomach.
3. Holozoic nutrition is a characteristic feature of all higher organisms. Justify taking the example of man.
4. Explain how plants acquire raw materials required for photosynthesis.
5. Enumerate all the events of digestion in human stomach and small intestine.
6. Name the digestive enzymes for fat digestion in gastric, pancreatic and intestinal juices. Mention the substrate on which they act and products formed.
7. Complete the following table:

	Organ	Enzyme present in the digestive juice	Action of enzyme
a)	Mouth	_______	_______
b)	_______	pepsin	_______
c)	_______	_______	converts proteins to amino acids
d)	_______	_______	emulsifies fats
e)	_______	trypsin	_______

8. Draw a well labelled diagram of a section of leaf showing various tissues and chloroplasts.
9. Describe the process of nutrition in *Amoeba* with the help of diagrams.
10. Give an account of main steps in the process of photosynthesis.
11. Explain briefly the opening and closing of stomata with the help of suitable diagrams.
12. Discuss the role played by chlorophyll in photosynthesis.
13. Mention the major glands associated with the alimentary canal of man and their functions.
14. How and in what form are the various components of food absorbed in the body?
15. Describe an activity to show that CO_2 is necessary for photosynthesis.
16. Answer the following:
    (a) Which is the first simple molecule of food produced by photosynthesis?
    (b) Why should the leaves be boiled in water before putting them in alcohol for testing of starch?

(c) Why a plant should be kept in dark during experiments on photosynthesis?

17. Describe digestion of carbohydrates in the alimentary canal of man.
18. Elaborate the main steps of photosynthesis.
19. Draw a well labelled diagram of site of exchange of gases in plants.
20. Draw a well labelled diagram of human digestive system showing following parts:

a. Mouth	b. Oesophagus
c. Stomach	d. Small intestine
e. Large intestine	f. Liver.

TEST YOURSELF

Fill in the blanks

1. *Amoeba* engulfs food by the process of ______.
2. Salivary amylase is also known as ______.
3. Finger-like projections are present in the ______ of man and are called as ______ which help in absorption of food.
4. The secretions of liver are stored in ______.
5. The protein digesting enzymes, pepsin and trypsin act in ______ and ______ medium respectively.
6. The digestive enzymes of *Amoeba* are stored in ______.
7. In man, protein digestion begins in ______.
8. ______ is the largest gland associated with alimentary canal in the human body.

Multiple-Choice Questions

Choose the correct option.

1. The type of nutrition in which organism feeds on dead and decaying matter is called
   (a) autotrophic (b) holozoic
   (c) saprophytic (d) parasitic

2. *Amoeba* captures food with the help of
   (a) cilia (b) tentacles
   (c) pseudopodia (d) mouth

3. Which of the following is not required for photosynthesis?
   (a) carbon dioxide (b) glucose
   (c) water (d) enzymes

4. Oxygen released in photosynthesis comes from
   (a) carbon dioxide (b) water
   (c) glucose (d) chlorophyll

5. Which among the following is a parasite?
   (a) leech (b) *amoeba*
   (c) housefly (d) fungi

6. While performing an experiment to show that chlorophyll is necessary for photosynthesis leaf is boiled in water. This is done to
   (a) remove chlorophyll
   (b) denature enzymes
   (c) make leaf soft
   (d) none of the above

7. Roundworm feeds upon
   (a) green leaves
   (b) dead and decayed matter
   (c) partly digested food
   (d) aquatic animals

8. Chlorophyll is a/an
   (a) gas (b) hormone
   (c) enzyme (d) pigment

9. The human saliva contains an enzyme ptyalin which digests
   (a) starch (b) proteins
   (c) sugars (d) fats

10. Which among the following is a vestigial organ?
    (a) colon (b) jejunum
    (c) vermiform appendix (d) pyloric

11. The autotrophic mode of nutrition requires
    (a) CO_2 and H_2O (b) chlorophyll
    (c) sunlight (d) all of the above

12. Tiny apertures found in the epidermis of leaf are called
    (a) lenticels (b) stomata
    (c) stroma (d) guard cells

13. Opening and closing of stomata is controlled by
    (a) age of leaf
    (b) turgidity of guard cells
    (c) amount of chloroplast present in the cells
    (d) hormonal changes in guard cells

14. The odd one out of the following is
    (a) round worm (b) hook worm
    (c) leech (d) tapeworm

15. Which is not a step of nutrition?
    (a) transportation (b) ingestion
    (c) digestion (d) egestion

16. Which of the following is not a digestive glands associated with the digestive system of man?
    (a) salivary glands (b) adrenal glands
    (c) liver (d) pancreas

Answers to Multiple-Choice Questions

1. (c)	2. (c)	3. (b)	4. (b)
5. (a)	6. (b)	7. (d)	8. (d)
9. (a)	10. (c)	11. (d)	12. (b)
13. (b)	14. (c)	15. (a)	16. (b)

2 RESPIRATION

Respiration and breathing

Respiration is a complex process. It includes breathing and cellular respiration.

- **Breathing** is the mechanism by which organisms obtain oxygen **(inhalation)** from the environment and release carbon dioxide **(exhalation)**.
- **Cellular respiration** is the process by which energy is produced by oxidation of digested food. It is a chemical process which takes place in cells. The cell organelle **mitochondrion** (plural mitochondria) is the site of respiration in cells. The energy released gets stored in ATP molecules.

  By **gaseous exchange**, oxygen reaches cells and carbon dioxide leave cells. Blood helps in the gaseous transport.

- **Aerobic respiraton** involves use of oxygen by cells to oxidise digested food substances (glucose) to release energy and carbon dioxide. The energy released from the oxidation of glucose gets stored in the form of ATP which powers the various life activities.

  Glucose $\longrightarrow$ Energy (ATP) + Carbon dioxide + Water

- **Anaerobic respiration** occurs in the absence of oxygen, in certain bacteria, yeast cells and also in our muscles during muscular activity. In this process in case of plants glucose gets converted into **ethanol** ('alcohol' in wines and beers) in the absence of oxygen. The production of alcohol (or other products) and energy by anaerobic respiration by yeast cells and certain bacteria is called **Fermentation**. Biotechnology exploits a range of fermentation reactions to produce different substances.

  Glucose $\longrightarrow$ Ethanol + Carbon dioxide + Energy

The diagram given below shows the links between breathing air, gaseous exchange and aerobic respiration in human beings.

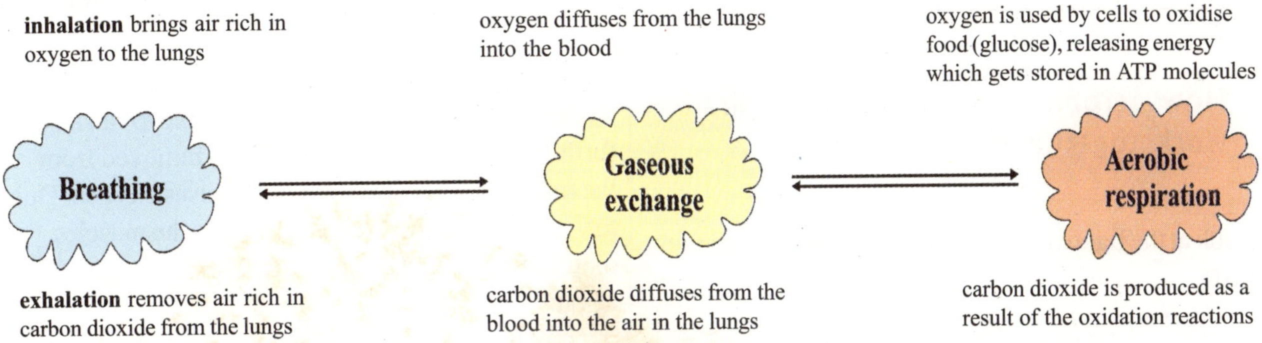

◆ **Glycolysis** is the process common to both aerobic and anaerobic respiration. It takes place in **cytoplasm** and does not require oxygen. In this process, the simple food glucose is converted to pyruvate.

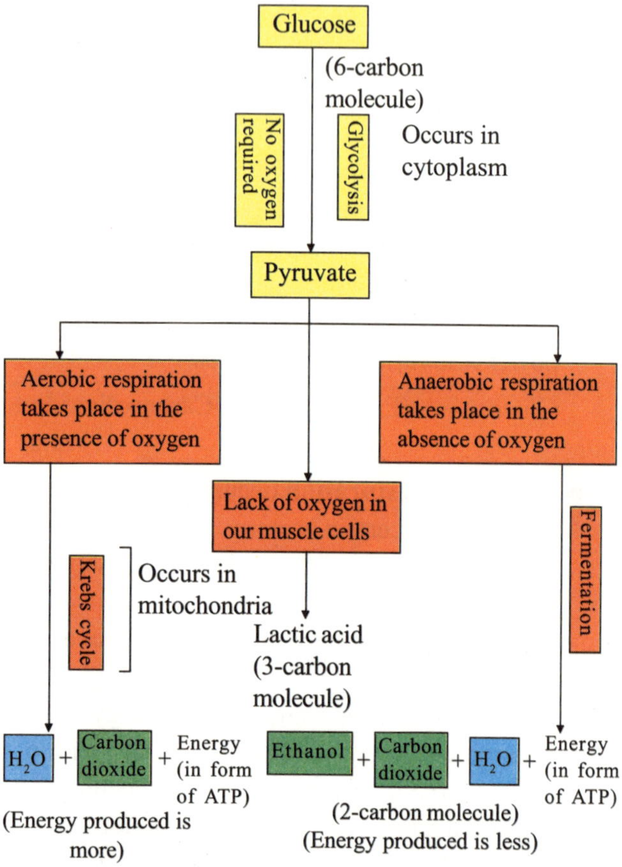

ATP is the energy currency. It is formed from ADP and inorganic phosphate.

$$\text{ADP} + \text{Ⓟ (Phosphate)} \xrightarrow{\text{energy}} \text{ADP} \sim \text{Ⓟ} = \text{ATP}$$

This ATP is broken using water thereby releasing 30.5 kJ/mol of energy.

How aerobic and anaerobic respiration work together?

Look at the figure given along with, the body is running fast.

The muscles of the boy are working hard. At first, aerobic respiration in the muscle cells starts and energy is released.

$$C_6H_{12}O_6 + 6O_2 \rightarrow 6CO_2 + 6H_2O$$

glucose + oxygen → carbon dioxide + water

energy released = 16.1 kJ/g glucose

The boy is panting and covered with sweat. However, in spite of rapid breathing and strenuous pumping by the heart, oxygen gets used up faster than it is available to muscle cells.

The muscles then switch from **aerobic respiration** to **anaerobic respiration** which does not use oxygen. **Lactic acid** is produced, which collects in the muscles.

glucose ⟶ lactic acid

energy released = 0.83 kJ/g glucose

Note that the energy released per gram of glucose is less in anaerobic and more in aerobic respiration.

As lactic acid accumulates, the muscles stop working. The boy feels tired and unable to run any further until the lactic acid has been removed from the muscles. This removal process uses oxygen. Due to vigorous panting, oxygen rushes to the muscles, oxidises lactic acid and aerobic respiration starts again.

Activity 1

1. Take some freshly prepared lime water in two bowls.
2. Blow air through the lime water in one of the bowls (a) and use a syringe or pichkari to pass air through the lime water in the other bowl (b).
3. Note how long it takes for the lime water to turn milky in both the bowls.

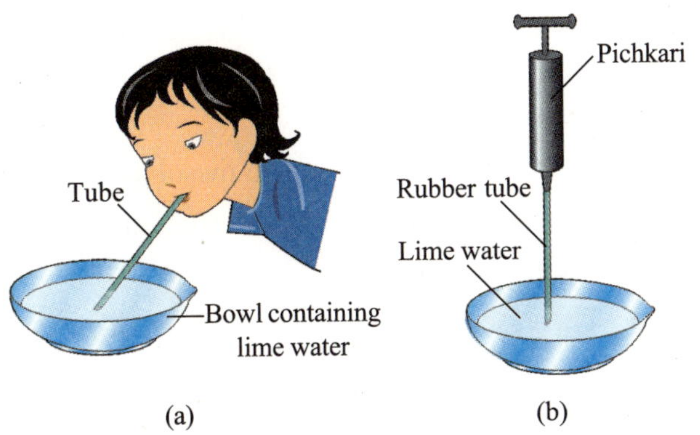

Lime water in the bowl (a), in which you blow through, will quickly turn milky. This is so because the air we exhale contains more carbon dioxide (than that in air we inhale).

Precautions

1. Lime water used should be freshly prepared for good result.
2. Breathe out strongly.

Fact File

Why is there a difference in energy output between aerobic respiration and anaerobic respiration?

- During aerobic respiration glucose (6-carbon molecule) is completely oxidised to carbon dioxide (1-carbon molecule) and water, releasing all of the available energy from each glucose molecule.
- During anaerobic respiration glucose is incompletely oxidised and ethanol or lactic acid is formed. Molecules of ethanol in plants and that of lactic acid in animals represent a considerable store of chemical bond energy. This energy is released only when the substances are oxidised aerobically.

The energy released during respiration enables:

- cells to make (synthesise) larger molecules from the combination of smaller ones.
- muscle cells to contract.
- mammals (including humans) and birds to maintain a steady body temperature even when the temperature of the surroundings changes.
- many endothermic reactions to take place in cells.

Questions

1. Differentiate between aerobic and anaerobic respiration. (3 marks)
2. Name two organisms which carry out anaerobic respiration. (2 marks)
3. Define respiration. (1 mark)

Respiration in plants

- The gaseous exhange between plants and the atmosphere occurs by diffusion through stomata and the large intercellular spaces.
- **Stomata** are tiny apertures on the surface of leaf. Oxygen diffuses in through stomata and finds its way into cells of the leaf.

- Oxygen present in between the soil particles, diffuses into root hairs and passes into other cells of the root.
- Carbon dioxide moves out into the soil from root cells.
  - During the day, primarily oxygen is released by plants as carbon dioxide produced by respiration is used up in photosynthesis.
  - At night, since photosynthesis stops, mainly carbon dioxide is eliminated out.

How respiration in plants, differs from that in animals?

- Respiration in plants occurs at a much slower rate than in animals.
- Unlike animals, there is little transport of gases from one part of the plant to another.
- All parts of a plant, like the root, stem and leaf perform respiration individually.

Questions

1. Differentiate between respiration and photosynthesis. (3 marks)
2. What is the function of stomata in leaves? (2 marks)

Exchange of gases in animals

1 ◆ In small organisms like *Amoeba* and *Hydra,* the exchange of gases occurs through the general body surface or cell membrane.

- Terrestrial animals breathe in the oxygen present in air.
  - The oxygen is either absorbed or allowed to enter through different organs in different animals.
- The common features of respiratory organs are
  - Generally they have large surface area to maximise exchange.
  - The surface is fine and delicate to facilitate easy exchange of gases.
  - They have rich blood supply as in humans.
  - For example, grasshopper, a terrestrial animal has a system of air tubes for exchange of gases, known as **tracheal system**.

2 ◆ **Earthworm** inhabits burrows in damp soil.

- Gaseous exchange occurs in it through the moist skin which absorbs oxygen and release carbon dioxide. It is also called as **cutaneous respiration**.
- Aquatic animals breathe in air dissolved in water.
  - **Fish** have gills adapted for efficient gaseous exchange in water.
  - The gaseous exchange depends on diffusion processes.
  - Due to the difference in the concentration gradients of oxygen and carbon dioxide between blood and water, exchange of gases takes place.
  - Rate of breathing in aquatic animals is much faster than that seen in terrestrial animal as the amount of dissolved oxygen is fairly low compared to the amount of oxygen in the air. Aquatic animals need to spend more energy so that more oxygen is able to pass over the respiratory surfaces.
  - Other aquatic animals like prawns and mussels also have gills as respiratory organs.

3 ◆ Frog lives both on land and in water.

- The respiratory organs in frog are skin and lungs.
- The skin is moist with a capillary network just below the surface and is capable of gas exchange either with air or water.

4 ◆ The respiratory organs in lizards, birds and humans are the lungs.

Questions

1. Name the organs responsible for respiration in fish. (1 mark)
2. Why is a terrestrial organism at advantage over an aquatic organism as regard to obtaining oxygen for respiration? (2 marks)

Respiration in human beings

The numbers on the concept map on page 22 refer to the checklist below.

Checklist for breathing, gaseous exchange and respiration

1 ◆ The **upper respiratory tract** consists of tubes from external nostrils through which air is inhaled.

- The tubes are well supplied with blood.

  As a result, inhaled air is warmed to body temperature.

◆ The external nostrils open into nasal cavities.

- The nasal cavity (air passage) is separated from oral cavity (food passage) by a bony palate.

  As a result, we can breathe in air even while we eat.

- Hairs in the nasal passage filter out large dust particles.
- The lining of **mucus** in the nasal cavity traps bacteria, viruses and dust particles.
- The nasal cavity ends in internal nostrils.
- Hair-like **cilia** sweep the mucus into the **pharynx**, where it is either swallowed, sneezed out or coughed up.

  As a result, the air entering the lungs is cleaned and made free from disease-causing micro-organisms.

◆ From nasal cavities, air enters pharynx which leads to **trachea** (windpipe).

2 ◆ Trachea is supported by L-shaped incomplete rings of cartilage which do not allow it to collapse when there is not much air in it.

◆ Trachea runs down the neck and divides into **bronchi** (singular bronchus), which lead into lungs. The bronchi further branch into many bronchioles.

- **Larynx** or voice box is an enlarged part of trachea covered by pieces of cartilage to form a box. Two vocal cords are stretched across the larynx which vibrate to produce sound.
- Each bronchiole terminates in a balloon-like sac called **alveolus** (plural **alveoli**).

◆ The millions of **alveoli** in a pair of human lungs form a surface area of about 90 m^2.

As a result, gaseous exchange is very efficient.

3 ◆ Gases diffuse rapidly across the wall of each alveolus because each wall is:

- **thin,** and therefore not a barrier to the rapid diffusion of gases.
- **moist;** gases dissolve in the layer of moisture and diffuse in solution.
- **well supplied with capillaries,** gases are quickly carried away from the alveoli in the bloodstream. The concentration gradient of gases between the blood and the air in the alveoli is steep.
- Blood supplies oxygen to the tissues and carbon dioxide from the tissues to the alveoli of lungs for exhalation. The respiratory pigment in the blood is **haemoglobin** which helps in transport of respiratory gases.
- Haemoglobin has a very high affinity for oxygen which is present in red blood

BREATHING, GASEOUS EXCHANGE AND RESPIRATION

CHECK LIST 1

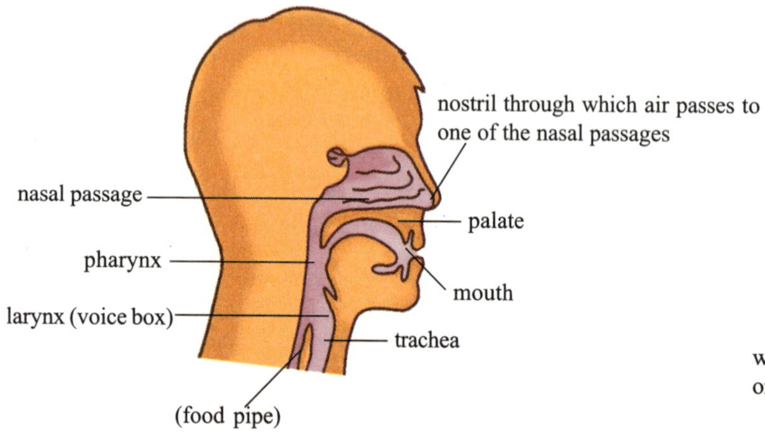

The respiratory tract

CHECK LIST 3

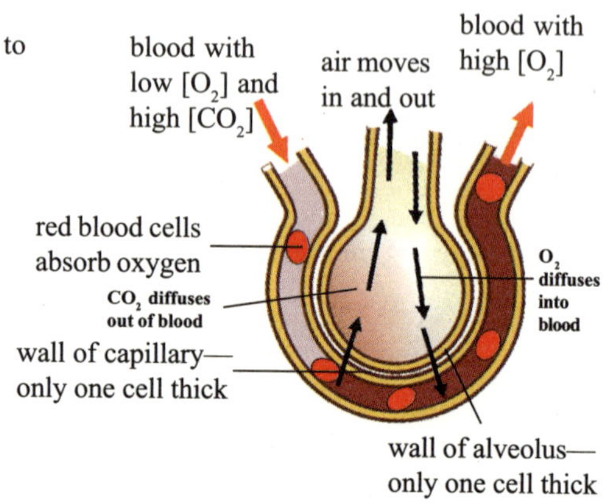

Alveolus movement of CO_2 and O_2

CHECK LIST 2

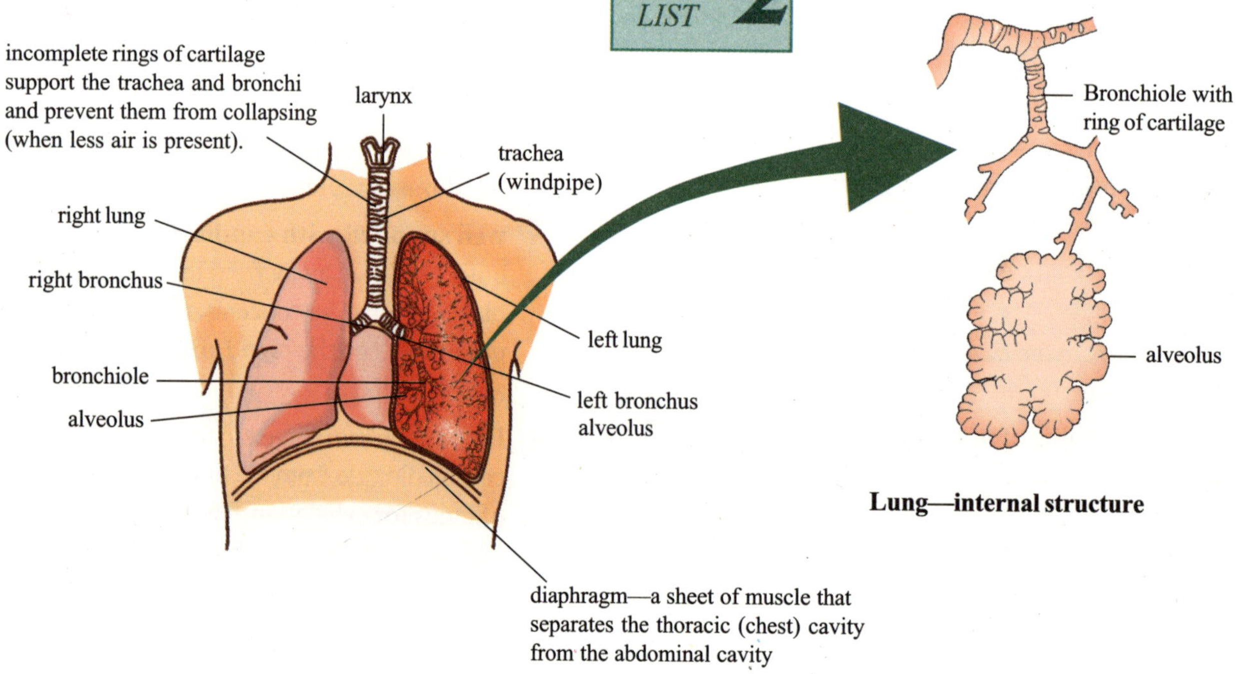

Lung—internal structure

corpuscles. Carbon dioxide is more soluble in water than oxygen is and mostly transported in the dissolved form in our blood.

- Haemoglobin is the respiratory pigment present in blood of human beings. It has a very high affinity for oxygen. If its amount reduces from the normal, less oxygen will be supplied to the tissues in the body. The individual may get tired very soon, while doing daily chores.

Breathing movements

- Breathing movements are involuntary, its rate is controlled by the respiratory centre of the brain.
- The lungs lie in the **thoracic cavity**.
- Thoracic cavity is separated from the abdominal cavity by a **diaphragm** (muscular partition).
- The **ribs** and **diaphragm** together form an elastic cage around the lungs. As they move, the pressure in the lungs changes.
  - This change in pressure causes **inhaling** (breathing in) and **exhaling** (breathing out).

Inhaling The volume of the thoracic cavity increases. The pressure of air inside the thoracic cavity becomes less than the atmospheric pressure, so air passes into the lungs. This is also called **inspiration**.

Exhaling The volume of the thoracic cavity decreases. The pressure of air inside the thoracic cavity becomes greater than atmospheric pressure, so air passes out of the lungs. This is also called **expiration**.

- During breathing cycle, when air is taken in and let out lungs always contain a residual volume of air so that there is sufficient time for oxygen to be absorbed and for carbon dioxide to be released.

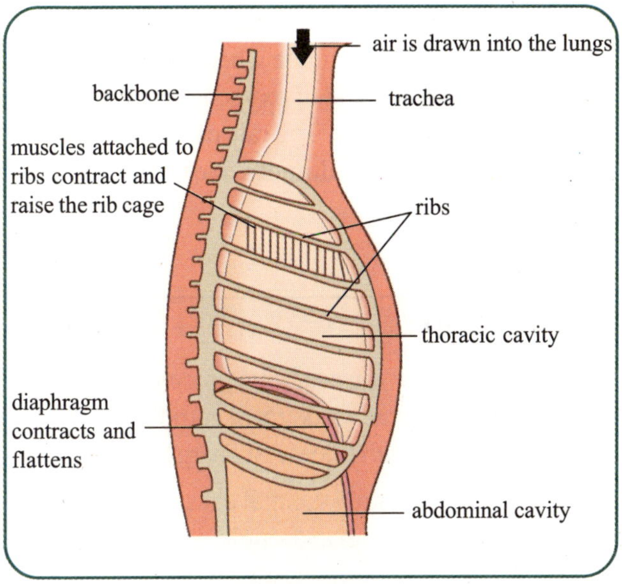

Inhalation

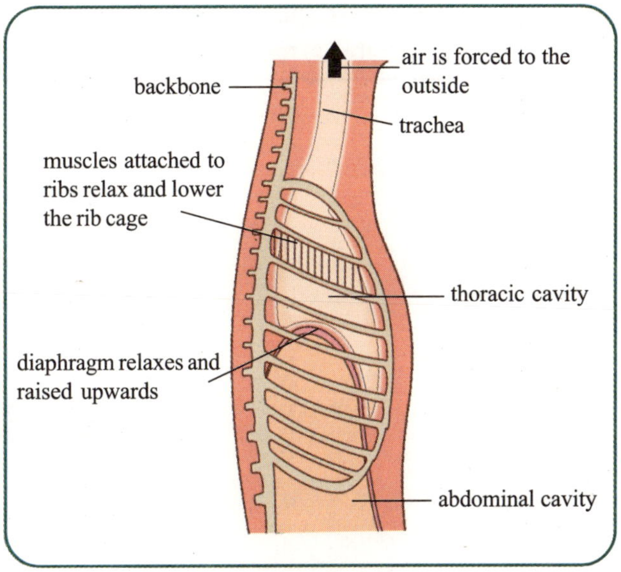

Exhalation

Did you know?

If oxygen had to move in our body only through diffusion it would take three years for a molecule of oxygen to get to our toes from our lungs. Haemoglobin makes it possible for oxygen to reach every cell quickly.

◆ During normal conditions the rate of breathing is 15 to 18 times per minute whereas during exercise the demand of oxygen increases the rate by 20–25 times. The rate of respiration also increases at higher altitudes due to lack of oxygen.

Remember

* Respiration is a catabolic process i.e., it involves breaking down of complex food materials with release of energy.
* All cells respire—animal cells, plant cells and the cells of fungi and single-celled organisms.
* Most cells respire aerobically.
* Some cells, such as muscle cells, the cells of plant roots, yeast cells and some types of bacteria, are able to respire anaerobically.

Questions

1. What will happen if the amount of haemoglobin decreases in blood? (1 mark)
2. How does the structure of alveoli help in maximising the exchange of gases? (1 mark)
3. Explain the transportation of respiratory gases in human beings. (2 marks)
4. Trace the route of the air into the lungs in humans. (3 marks)

EXERCISES

I. Very Short Answer Questions

(1 mark)

1. Define respiration.
2. 'The rate of respiration in plants is less than that in animals.' Suggest one reason for it.
3. What are the two types of respiration?
4. Which is more efficient—aerobic or anaerobic respiration?
5. What is the site of cellular respiration?
6. What is the energy currency of the cell?
7. What are the two main steps of respiration?
8. What is the end product of glycolysis?

9. Name the compound that enters Krebs cycle.
10. What are the products of anaerobic respiration?
11. In which tissues of human body anaerobic respiration takes place?
12. Name an organism which respires by skin.
13. What are the products of aerobic respiration?
14. Where does glycolysis occurs in a cell?
15. Name an organism that respires without oxygen.
16. What are alveoli?
17. Which substrate is oxidised in the cell during respiration?
18. What is the role of mucus membrane present inside the nasal passage?
19. What is the advantage of having hairs in the nasal cavity?
20. Name the respiratory organs of fish.
21. What is the rate of breathing in humans under normal conditions?
22. Name the pores in the leaf through which respiratory exchange of gases take place.
23. Why the walls of trachea do not collapse when there is less air in it?
24. Find the odd one out:
    bronchus, diaphragm, trachea, alveolus.
25. Which process is common to both aerobic and anaerobic respiration?
26. What happens to the breathing rate during exercise?
27. Give an example of anaerobic process useful in biotechnology.
28. What is the common passage for both food and air in man?
29. Define fermentation.
30. Why do the divers carry oxygen with them?
31. Name two animal groups that respire through lungs.
32. Name the respiratory organ of earthworm.
33. Define breathing.
34. What happens when lactic acid accumulates in muscles of human beings?
35. What happens when diaphragm and muscles attached to ribs contract?
36. Name the muscular partition that separates thoracic cavity from abdominal cavity.
37. Name the respiratory gases.
38. Which physical phenomenon makes exchange of gases possible in plants?
39. What does the following reaction represent?
    Glucose $\rightarrow$ Pyruvate $\rightarrow CO_2 + H_2O$ + Energy
40. Which gas is present in large amount in blood vessels coming out from lungs?
41. What is cutaneous respiration?
42. Write the overall reaction for complete oxidation of glucose molecule.
43. How much energy is released from the breakdown of one molecule of glucose?
44. How does single-celled organisms like *Amoeba* respire?
45. Why is breathing through nose healthier?

II. Short Answer Questions

(2 marks)

1. How breathing is different from respiration?
2. Where exactly does oxidation of glucose takes place during respiration and in which form energy is released?
3. What happens to the rate of breathing during vigorous excerise and why?
4. Why does the rate of respiration increases at higher altitude?
5. What is the role of diaphragm during inhalation and exhalation?

6. What happens to carbon dioxide that collects in tissues in the human body?
7. 'Even if there is more oxygen in the air, fish die when taken out of water.' Give reasons.
8. Why is there no respiratory pigment in the blood of insects?
9. Why are alveoli surrounded by blood capillaries?
10. What are the disadvantages of respiring through mouth?
11. Why *Amoeba* does not need any respiratory system?
12. Why more amount of energy is produced during aerobic respiration?
13. Where is larynx located? What is its function?
14. How does blood help in respiration?
15. How do ciliated and mucus cells in trachea assist in the process of respiration?
16. How anaerobic respiration in yeast cells differs from that of body muscles in man?
17. Why is rate of breathing faster in aquatic animals?
18. What are vocal cords and what is its function?
19. Show correct sequence of movement of air in the following:
    surroundings, blood, blood vessel, air sac, bronchus, nose, nasal cavity.
20. How respiration in plants is different during day and night time?
21. Why respiration in plants occurs at a much slower rate than that in animals?
22. How is transportation of oxygen different from carbon dioxide?
23. How are the alveoli designed to maximise the exchange of gases?
24. What would happen if diffusion would have been the only way to move oxygen through our body?

III. Short Answer Questions

(3 marks)

1. Differentiate between aerobic and anaerobic respiration.
2. 'Do active tissues have rapid respiration?' Give reasons in support of your answer.
3. How gaseous exchange takes place between tissues and blood?
4. Identify the type of respiration from the end-products formed:
    (a) Ethanol and CO_2
    (b) CO_2 and H_2O
    (c) Lactic acid
5. What are the major organs of respiratory system in man?
6. List the main functions of the respiratory system.
7. If one holds his breath for about 30 seconds after expiration, would there still be any exchange of gases occurring in the lungs? Explain giving reasons.
8. What special features make skin an effective respiratory organ in some animals? Give example of an animal respiring through skin.
9. Why do higher organisms require more extensive respiratory surface?
10. How is respiration carried out in lower organisms?
11. Give a diagrammatic respresentation of exchange of gases between blood capillaries and tissue cells.
12. Differentiate between respiration and photosynthesis.
13. Enumerate the three basic properties associated with a respiratory surface.
14. How are lungs designed in man to maximise the area for exchange of gases?

15. Why more amount of energy is produced during aerobic respiration?
16. What are the factors that influence rate of respiration?
17. Give reasons.
    (a) Lactic acid accumulates in muscles during the course of heavy exercise.
    (b) Air from outside becomes moist and warm before it reaches lungs.

IV. Long Answer Questions

(5 marks)

1. 'Respiration is a vital function of the body.' Justify.
2. Discuss the mechanism of inspiration and expiration in humans.
3. Discuss the characteristics of respiratory tract in humans.
4. Explain the overall process of respiration with the help of a schematic diagram.
5. Describe the structure of lungs in man, with the help of a suitable diagram.
6. Explain briefly respiration in plants.
7. Explain the process of gaseous exchange in human beings.
8. Draw a well labelled diagram of the human respiratory system.
9. Explain the role of various parts of respiratory system in man.
10. How is pyruvic acid or pyruvate produced in a cell? What is its function in the cell?
11. Why do we say respiration is the reversal of photosynthesis? Explain.
12. How does the gaseous exchange between tissue and blood takes place?

TEST YOURSELF

Fill in the blanks

1. The common pathway of aerobic and anaerobic respiration is ______.
2. ______ is another name for windpipe.
3. Each ______ terminates in an alveolar sac in lungs.
4. In animals, the end-product of anaerobic respiration is ______.
5. Oxygen is carried by ______ in the blood.
6. The lungs occupy most of the ______ cavity in the human body.
7. During respiration, pyruvic acid enters the mitochondria, if ______ is available.
8. Larynx is a passageway between ______ and ______.

Multiple-Choice Questions

Choose the correct option.

1. The energy rich compound produced during respiration is
   (a) ATP (b) ADP
   (c) glucose (d) NADP

2. The final product of glycolysis is
   (a) lactic acid (b) glucose
   (c) pyruvic acid (d) RuBP

3. Which of the following does not respire through lungs?
   (a) whale (b) frog
   (c) dog (d) earthworm

4. Which of the following has air tubes reaching different parts of the body?
   (a) earthworm (b) grasshopper
   (c) starfish (d) crab

5. The end product of anaerobic respiration in plants is
   (a) ethyl alcohol (b) lactic acid
   (c) CO_2 (d) O_2

6. Lactic acid formation occurs during
   (a) anaerobic respiration in muscles
   (b) anaerobic respiration in yeast
   (c) aerobic respiration in muscles
   (d) aerobic respiration in yeast

7. Krebs cycle is a part of
   (a) glycolysis (b) aerobic respiration
   (c) anaerobic respiration (d) fermentation

8. Vocal cords are present in
   (a) glottis (b) pharynx
   (c) larynx (d) trachea

9. Muscular partition that separates thoracic cavity from abodominal cavity is called
   (a) pleura (b) diaphragm
   (c) alveoli (d) pericardium

10. The site of gaseous exchange in lungs is
    (a) bronchi (b) bronchioles
    (c) alveoli (d) trachea

11. Respiration is the reverse of
    (a) transpiration (b) breathing
    (c) photosynthesis (d) combustion

12. Respiration uses
    (a) electrical energy (b) chemical energy
    (c) solar energy (d) mechanical energy

13. Breathing is a __________ process.
    (a) biochemical (b) mechanical
    (c) chemical (d) physical

14. Which of the following solutions is used to test the presence of CO_2?
    (a) lime water (b) alcohol
    (c) glucose water (d) salt solution

15. The cell organelle associated with cellular respiration is
    (a) golgi complex (b) endoplasmic reticulum
    (c) mitochondrion (d) lysosome

16. Respiration is
    (a) catabolic (b) anabolic
    (c) both a and b (d) none of these

17. Respiratory surfaces in animals
    (a) are thin and delicate
    (b) have large surface area
    (c) have rich blood supply
    (d) all of the above

18. The openings on the surface of leaf that allow gaseous exchange are
    (a) stomata (b) nostrils
    (c) epidermis (d) cuticle

19. Glycolysis process
    (a) does not need O_2
    (b) needs O_2
    (c) needs CO_2
    (d) none of these

Answers to Multiple-Choice Questions

1. (a)	2. (c)	3. (d)	4. (b)
5. (a)	6. (a)	7. (b)	8. (c)
9. (b)	10. (c)	11. (c)	12. (b)
13. (d)	14. (a)	15. (c)	16. (a)
17. (d)	18. (a)	19. (a)	

3 TRANSPORTATION

All cells in the body of living organisms require food and water to survive. In a multicellular organism, materials are transported to and from individual cells in all parts of the organism. As a result, efficient means of internal transport have evolved in organisms.

Transport of materials in plants

- The raw materials needed by plants to carry on the process of photosynthesis in green leaves are carbon dioxide, water and minerals, and sunlight.
- Except for carbon dioxide (which is taken in through pores in leaves), the nearest and richest source of raw materials is soil.
- The minerals dissolved in water are transported to leaves, from soil through roots (roots are the only plant organs in touch with the soil).
- If the plant body is small, the process of transportation of minerals and water can be easily done by diffusion.
- Transportation by diffusion is not possible, when the plant body is large; for example, in tall trees like mango, eucalyptus etc.
- Energy needs differ between different body designs.
- Since plants do not move and dead tissues constitute a substantial part of the plant body, energy needs of plants are less than that of animals.

  As a result, slow transport systems can work in plants.
- Plants need two conducting tissues to move food (energy reserves) from leaves and raw materials from roots.
- The conducting tissues of plants are xylem and phloem.
- Water and minerals are absorbed from the soil by roots and transported to the other parts of the plant like stem, leaves and flowers through **xylem**.
- Food (sugar) synthesized by the leaves is transported to the other parts of the plant through **phloem**.

☞ **Remember**

* The exchange of water vapour and carbon dioxide between the inside of the leaf and the atmosphere takes place through **stomata**. The loss of water vapour from the leaf is called **transpiration**.

The numbers on the concept map on pages 34–35 refer to the checklist of points below.

Checklist for transport in plants

1 ◆ There are two kinds of xylem elements which take part in the transport process—tracheids and vessels. Both these elements consist of dead cells.

- **Tracheids** are long, thin, spindle-shaped cells. The thick cell walls have pits through which water flows from one tracheid to another.
- **Vessels** are made up of a series of long cells joined end to end. Mature xylem vessels have no living contents and their end walls have broken down.

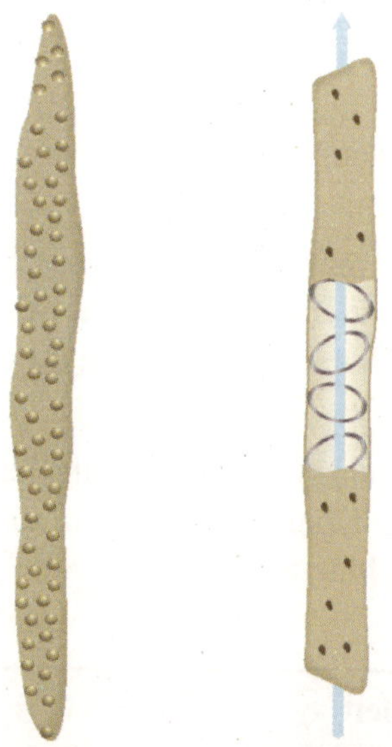

Xylem elements

- In non-flowering plants, tracheids are the only conducting cells whereas in flowering plants, both tracheids and vessels, or only vessels, conduct water.

◆ Minerals are taken up dissolved in water in the inorganic form such as nitrates and phosphates.

◆ Cells of root hair in contact with the soil actively take up ions which create a difference in ionic concentration between soil and root. Water therefore moves into the root to eliminate this difference.

◆ The walls of xylem tubes are waterproof, due to the presence of a substance called **lignin**.

◆ As water transpires, more is drawn from the xylem in the leaf.

As a result, water is 'sucked' upwards through the xylem of the stem.

In other words, transpiration is another main phenomenon which helps in the upward movement of sap or water from roots to leaves.

◆ Transpiration also helps in temperature regulation.

As a result, more water is supplied to the bottom of the xylem by the roots. Thus, unbroken moving columns of water from the roots to the leaves are formed. This is a **passive transport** i.e., no energy is used in transportation.

◆ Another important process which plays an important role in transport of water especially at night is **root pressure**, as transpiration does not occur at night.

2 ◆ Phloem consists of living cells. It consists of sieve tubes and companion cells.

- Sieve tube elements are joined end to end to form a system of tubes that runs throughout the plant. Perforated sieve plates are present at both the openings of tubes. Companion cells are small with thin walls. Phloem transports sugars (mainly sucrose) and other substances (like amino acids) formed as a result of metabolic reactions and hormones (synthesised at the shoot and root tips) to other parts of the plant. These substances are especially transported to the storage organs of roots, fruits and seed and to growing organs. The process is called **translocation**.

- Translocation of food and other substances in phloem requires energy from ATP.
  - This increases the osmotic pressure of the phloem tissue causing water to move into it. This pressure moves the material in the phloem to other tissues with less pressure. This is how movement of food materials takes place according to the needs of the plant.

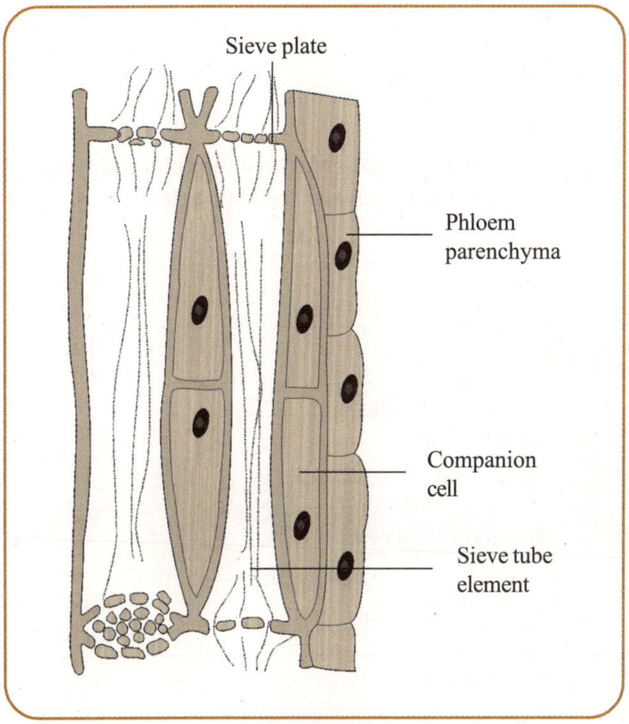

Phloem tissue

- During spring season, sugar stored in root or stem tissue is transported to the buds which need energy to grow.

Did you know that on an average a tree transpires water equivalent to 100 times its weight in its lifetime. Water in some flowering plant rises at the rate of 10 to 100 cm per minute during the day.

Activity 1

1. Take a potted plant and cover it with a transparent plastic sheet.
2. Keep the plant in bright sunlight for about half an hour.
3. You will observe tiny droplets of water on the inside of the plastic sheet.

   Due to the plastic sheet cover, the water transpired by plants cannot escape into the air, and is thus seen as tiny droplets.

Questions

1. What are the raw materials transported in plants? (2 marks)
2. Why the transport system is slow in plants? (1 mark)
3. What do you mean by the term 'translocation'? (1 mark)
4. Why do plants have low energy needs? (2 marks)
5. Why is that the effect of root pressure in transport of water is more important at night? (2 marks)

Transportation in human beings

The substances which are to be transported in the human body to relevant organs are digested food, oxygen, hormones and excretory products. The conducting tissues in the human body are **blood** and **lymph**.

TRANSPORT OF WATER

Transpiration helps in the upward movement of water from roots to leaves.

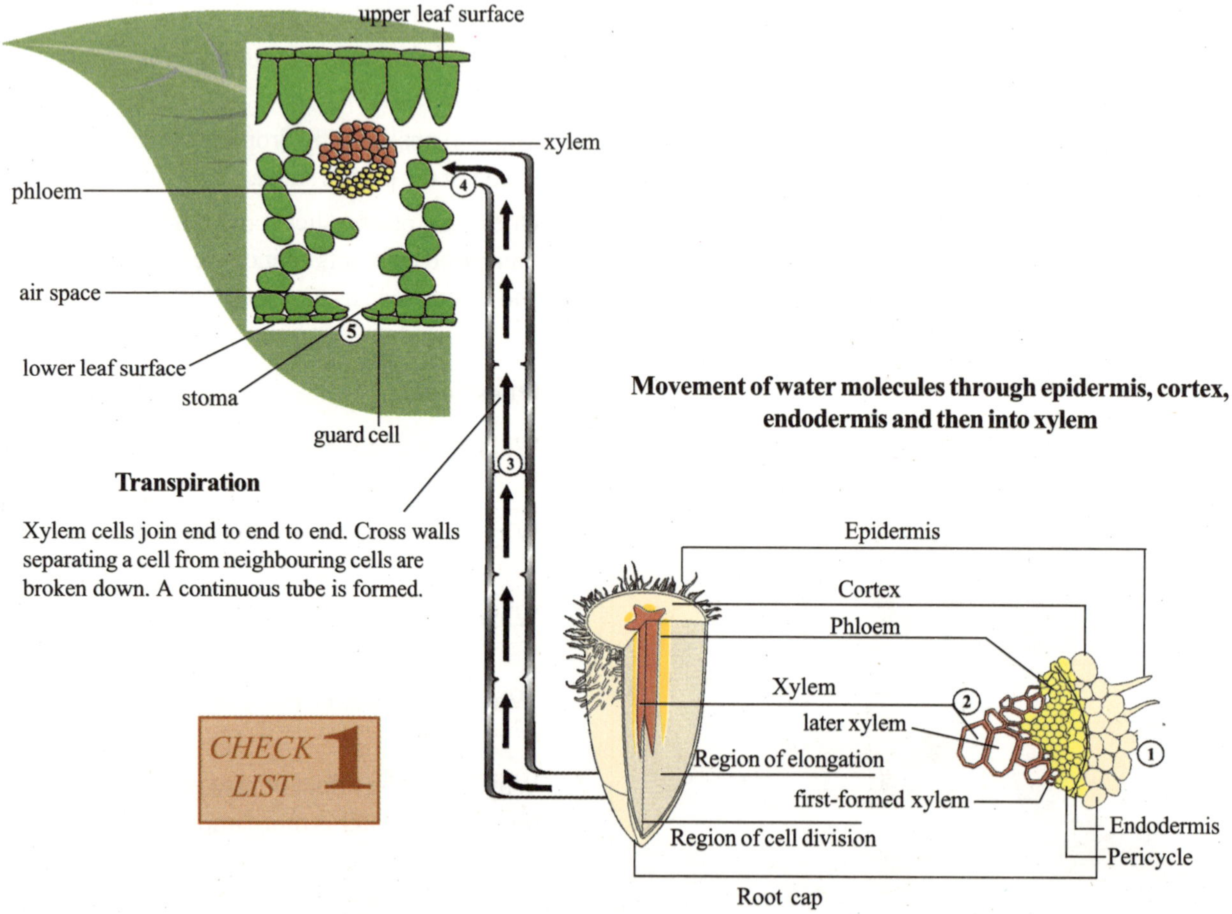

Transpiration

Xylem cells join end to end to end. Cross walls separating a cell from neighbouring cells are broken down. A continuous tube is formed.

Movement of water molecules through epidermis, cortex, endodermis and then into xylem

Pathway of transport of water

Key→ See **1–5** and trace the path of water from roots to leaves.

① Root hairs absorb water and mineral ions from the soil by osmosis. Mineral ions are dissolved in water.

Root hairs are in close contact with the thin film of water surrounding the soil particles.

② Water and minerals dissolved in it move through root cortex, endodermis and reach the root xylem.

③ Water travels through the xylem of the root and stem in unbroken columns—the transpiration stream.

④ Water moves through the xylem of the leaf stalk and veins of the leaf.

About 1–2% of the water absorbed by the plant is used up in photosynthesis.

⑤ The concentration of water vapour in the atmosphere is lower than that in the air spaces of the leaf. Therefore it diffuses from the leaf through the stomata. The process is called **transpiration**.

Water lost by cells through evaporation is replaced with water drawn through the cells by osmosis. Cells next to the xylem draw water from the xylem by osmosis.

(→) Direction of water molecules moving upwards.

TRANSPORT OF FOOD

Food molecules enter the phloem cells from mesophyll cells of the leaf.

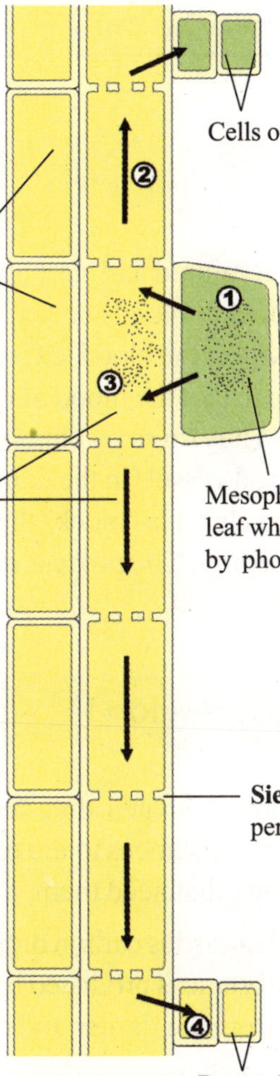

CHECK LIST 2

ASCENT OF WATER AND MINERALS IN PLANTS

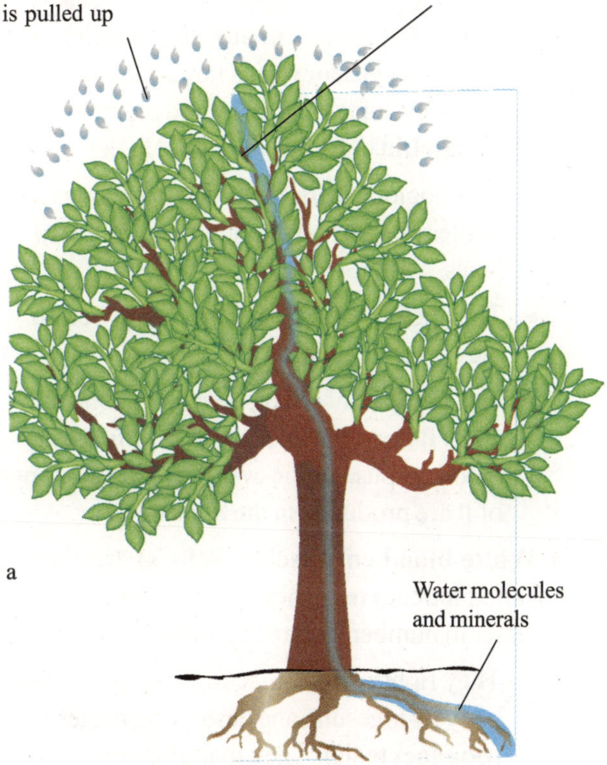

Pathway of transport of food

Key→ See 1–4 and trace the path of food from mesophyll cells of the leaf to the other parts of the plant.

① Sugar passes from the leaf cells into the sieve cells by **active transport**.

② Food or sugar molecules enter the sieve cells of phloem from where they are transported to all parts of the plant body **(translocation)**.

③ Due to high concentration of sugar in the sieve cell, water, is drawn in through osmosis. Thus food is transported in a dilute aqueous solution.

④ In some plants, food which reaches roots is stored in the form of starch.

Translocation is essential as every part of the plant needs food.

➔ movement of sugar and other dissolved substances

What is blood?

1 ◆ Blood is a connective tissue. It has fluid matrix called **plasma**. It carries three kinds of cells—red blood cells, white blood cells and platelets.

2 ◆ Plasma is the main transporting fluid in blood which transports food, carbon dioxide and nitrogenous wastes in dissolved form. It is a straw-coloured liquid and contains a lot of water and many proteins.

3 ◆ **Red blood cells or corpuscles (RBCs)** are also called **erythrocytes**. They are circular in shape. They contain red coloured pigment **haemoglobin** due to which blood looks red.

- Haemoglobin carries oxygen from lungs to tissues and carbon dioxide from tissues to lungs.
- The nuclei of red blood cells is lost before they enter circulation.
- The life span of red blood cells is about 120 days. It is estimated that three million red blood corpuscles die everyday but four times of it are produced in the bone marrow.

4 ◆ **White blood corpuscles (WBCs)** are also called **leucocytes**. They are nucleated and lesser in number than red blood cells.

- They fight against infection and protect the body by ingesting and destroying bacteria **(phagocytosis)**. They manufacture **antibodies** which act against foreign bodies or organisms.

  As a result, they are responsible for immunity of the body and are known as 'soldiers' of the body.

5 ◆ **Platelets** are the fragments of blood corpuscles which help in clotting of the blood. They do not possess nuclei.

Remember

- * Red blood corpuscles are produced in the marrow of the limb bones from stem cells.
- * Old red blood corpuscles are destroyed in the liver.
- * White blood corpuscles originate in the bone marrow and spleen.

Maintenance by platelets

What if we get injured and start bleeding? The unstoppable loss of blood can lead to death. Platelets present in the blood, circulating all through the body help to clot the blood at wounds and so stop the bleeding. They do so by clumping together at the cut end of blood vessel (in the damaged tissue) and thus forming a clot. This blocks the smaller capillaries and stops bleeding. The process occurs as a series of reactions in the blood.

Functions of blood

◆ Blood carries oxygen, digested food, hormones and other substances to the tissues and organs of the body that need them.

◆ Blood also carries carbon dioxide and other waste substances produced by the metabolism of cells from the tissues and organs of the body.

◆ Blood helps in temperature regulation of the body from the attack of foreign bodies and disease-causing pathogens.

◆ A **heart beat** has two phases—**systole** and **diastole**.

- In a systole, the ventricles **contract** and force blood into arteries.
- In a diastole, the ventricles **relax** and take in blood from the atria.

- In both the phases, pressure in the blood is different.
- The normal systolic pressure is about 120 mm of Hg and the normal diastolic pressure is 80 mm of Hg.

◆ Blood pressure is measured with an instrument called **sphygmomanometer**.

◆ The constriction of arterioles results in increased resistance to blood pressure. This is called **hypertension**. It can lead to the rupture of an artery and internal bleeding.

Human circulatory system

The circulatory system makes the blood reach all parts of the body. It consists of **heart** and **blood vessels**.

◆ The **heart** is a central pumping organ. It is a muscular organ as big as our closed fist.

◆ **Blood vessels** are tube-like through which blood flows.

heart —pumps→ **blood** —through→ **blood vessels**

Blood vessels are of three kinds arteries, veins and capillaries.

Arteries

- carry blood (at high pressure) away from the heart to organs and tissues.
- have a pulse because the vessel walls contract and relax as blood spurts from the heart.
- have thick and elastic walls.

Veins

- return blood (at low pressure) to the heart from organs and tissues (except hepatic portal vein).
- do not have a pulse since blood flows smoothly.
- have valves to ensure that blood flows only in one direction.
- are thin-walled.

Capillaries

- on reaching organ or tissue, arteries divide into smaller vessels called capillaries.
- exchange food material, gases and waste from tissues.
- are thin walled (one celled) and extremely narrow where exchange of materials between blood and surrounding cells takes place.
- occur at the terminals of artery and vein.

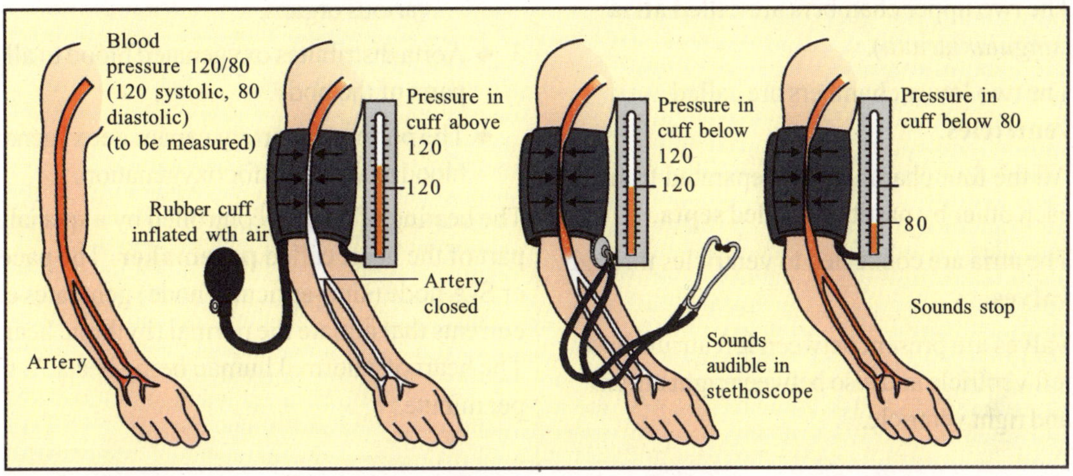

Activity 2

1. Visit a health centre in your locality and find the haemoglobin content in different age groups and sex.

Haemoglobin content	5–10 years	10–15 years	15–20 years	20–25 years
in males				
in females				

The normal range of haemoglobin content in

- children is ________
- adults is ________

Compare the content differences in males and females. Find why there are differences in haemoglobin content at different age groups and that in males and females.

The numbers on the concept map on pages 39–40 refer to the checklist of points below.

Checklist for the human heart

1 ◆ The human heart is four chambered. This prevents the oxygen-rich blood from mixing with the blood containing carbon dioxide.

- The two upper chambers are called **atria** (*singular* atrium).
- The two lower chambers are called **ventricles**.
- All the four chambers are separated from each other by partitions called **septa**.
- The atria are connected to ventricles through **valves**.
- Valves are present between left atrium and left ventricle and also between right atrium and right ventricle.
- Valves permit the flow of blood from atrium to ventricle and not in the reverse order.

2 ◆ Heart beats all the time throughout one's life.

- Heart (cardiac) muscle is special and contracts and relaxes rhythmically for a lifetime.

◆ When muscles of all the four chambers of the heart are relaxed

- the large veins called vena cava, pour blood into right atrium.
- vena cava carry deoxygenated blood from tissues which have used up all the oxygen.
- the pulmonary vein pours oxygenated blood into the left atrium.

◆ Next when the cardiac muscles contract, the contraction starts in atria and then passes to ventricles.

- When atria contract, right atrium pours deoxygenated blood into right ventricle and left atrium pours oxygenated blood into left ventricle.

◆ Next, when ventricles contract, the left ventricle pours oxygenated blood in largest artery called **aorta**.

- From the right ventricle, the deoxygenated blood flows into pulmonary artery.
- Ventricles have thicker muscular walls than the atria as they have to pump blood into various organs.

3 ◆ Aorta distributes oxygenated blood to all the parts of the body.

◆ The pulmonary artery carries deoxygenated blood to the lungs for oxygenation.

The beating of heart is controlled by a specialised part of the heart called **pacemaker**. The pacemaker or S-A node (sinu-auricular node) generates electric currents that initiate the normal rhythmic heartbeats. The heart of a normal human being beats 72 times per minute.

TRANSPORTATION IN THE HUMAN BODY

CHECK LIST 1

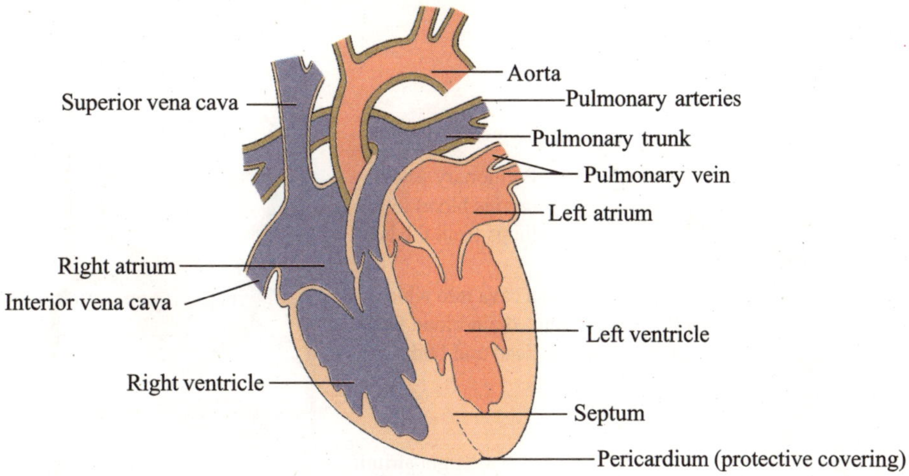

The Human heart

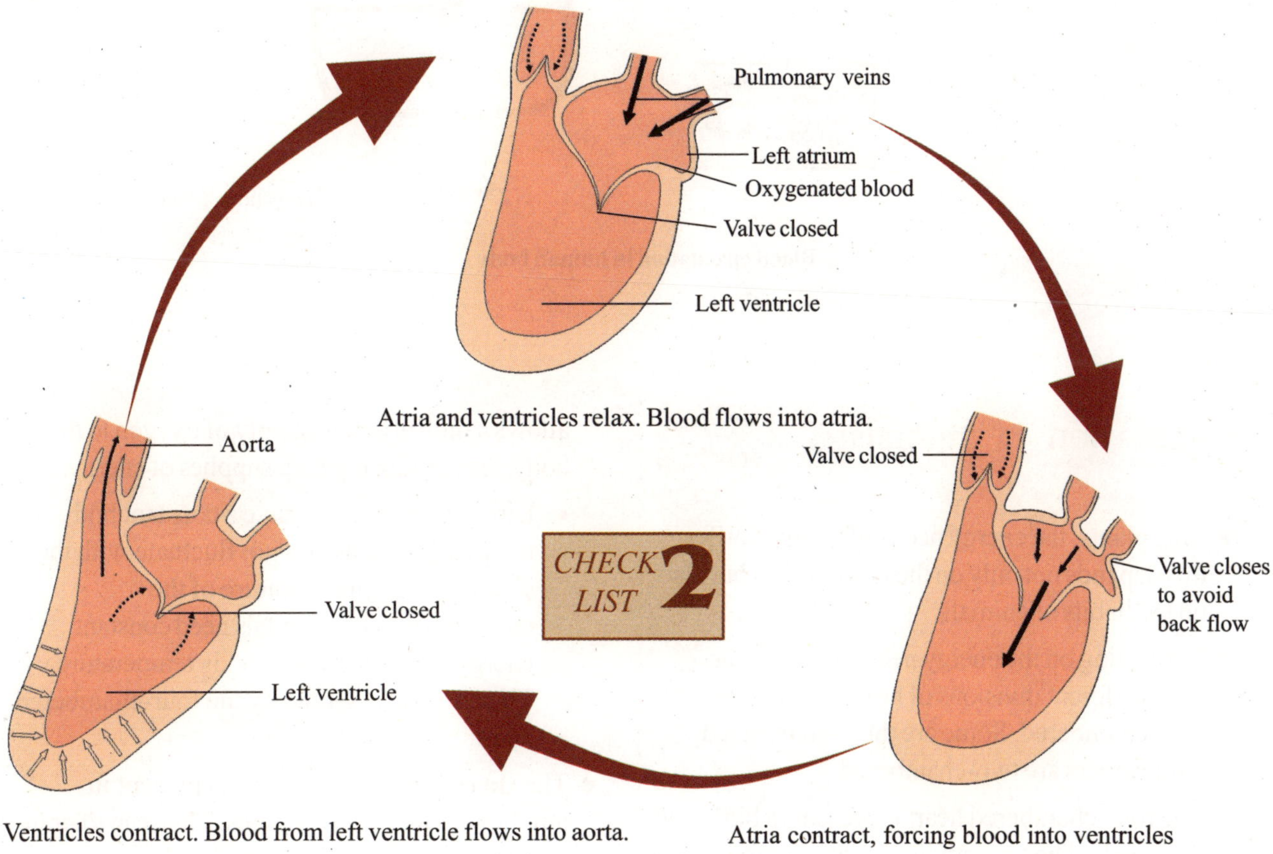

Events during heart beat

(**Note:** Illustrated by reference to the left side of the heart only.)

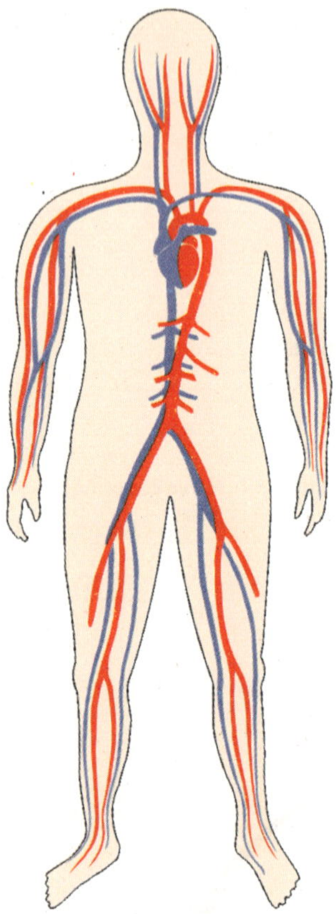

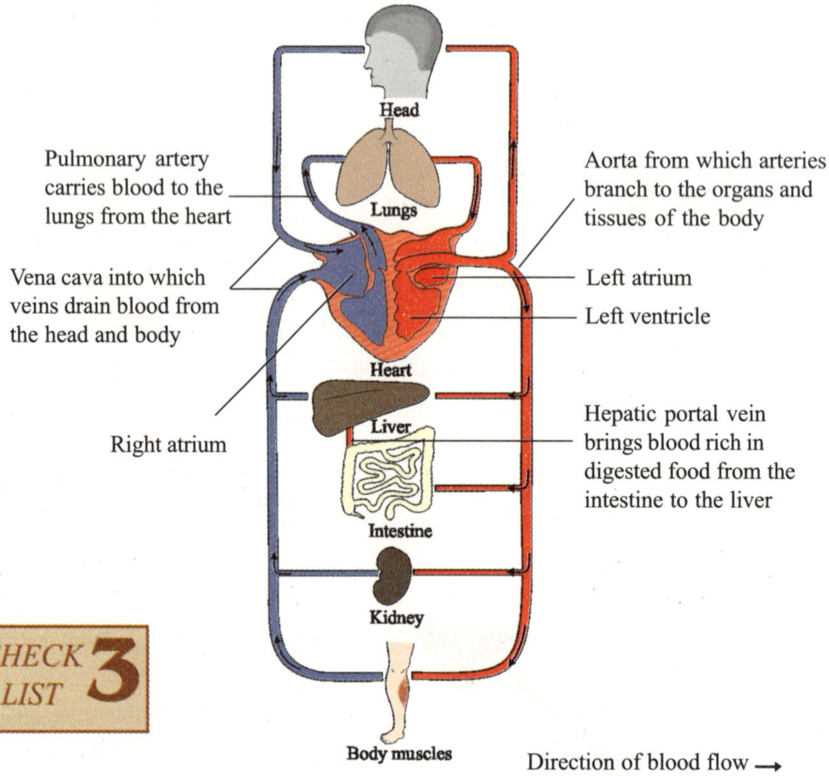

CHECK LIST 3

Blood circulation in human body

Circulation in animals

- Like plants, the energy needs of animals differ; this depends not only on the body design but also on the habits of animals.
- Depending on the energy needs, the animals have different divisions of heart. Not all are four-chambered. Some are three-chambered while others are two-chambered.
- The four-chambered heart is present in birds and mammals. The separation of heart into four chambers is useful to keep away oxygenated and deoxygenated blood from mixing. This allows a high efficient supply of oxygen to the body, thus producing high supplies of energy.
  - Birds and mammals have a constant body temperature that does not fluctuate with the changes in the temperature of the environment. The animals need constant energy to maintain their body temperature. The purpose is served by the four-chambered heart.
- The **three-chambered** heart is present in amphibians and many reptiles. They can tolerate some mixing of the oxygenated and deoxygenated blood due to their not so active life.

- Fish have only **two-chambered** heart. The blood is pumped to gills where it gets oxygenated to pass on directly to the rest of the body. Thus, blood is passed only once through the heart in one cycle of its passage through the whole body.
  - When blood passes twice through the heart in one cycle of its passage through the body, it is called as **double circulation**. It is found in animals with four-chambered and three-chambered hearts.

Double circulation is also found in human circulatory system because blood flows twice through the hearts.

How different materials in the blood reach individual cells?

Capillaries run close to all cells. Plasma of the blood passes out of capillaries to form the tissue fluid or lymph. Tissue fluid is a watery solution containing all the dissolved substances from the plasma that bathes the cells. It is also called extracellular fluid. The cells take up substances (such as oxygen and glucose) from the tissue fluid and pass waste products (such as carbon dioxide and urea) into the tissue fluid along concentration gradients.

Questions

1. What are the components of the transport system in humans? (1 mark)
2. Name the two conducting tissues in human body. (1 mark)
3. Why separation of heart into chambers is useful? (2 marks)

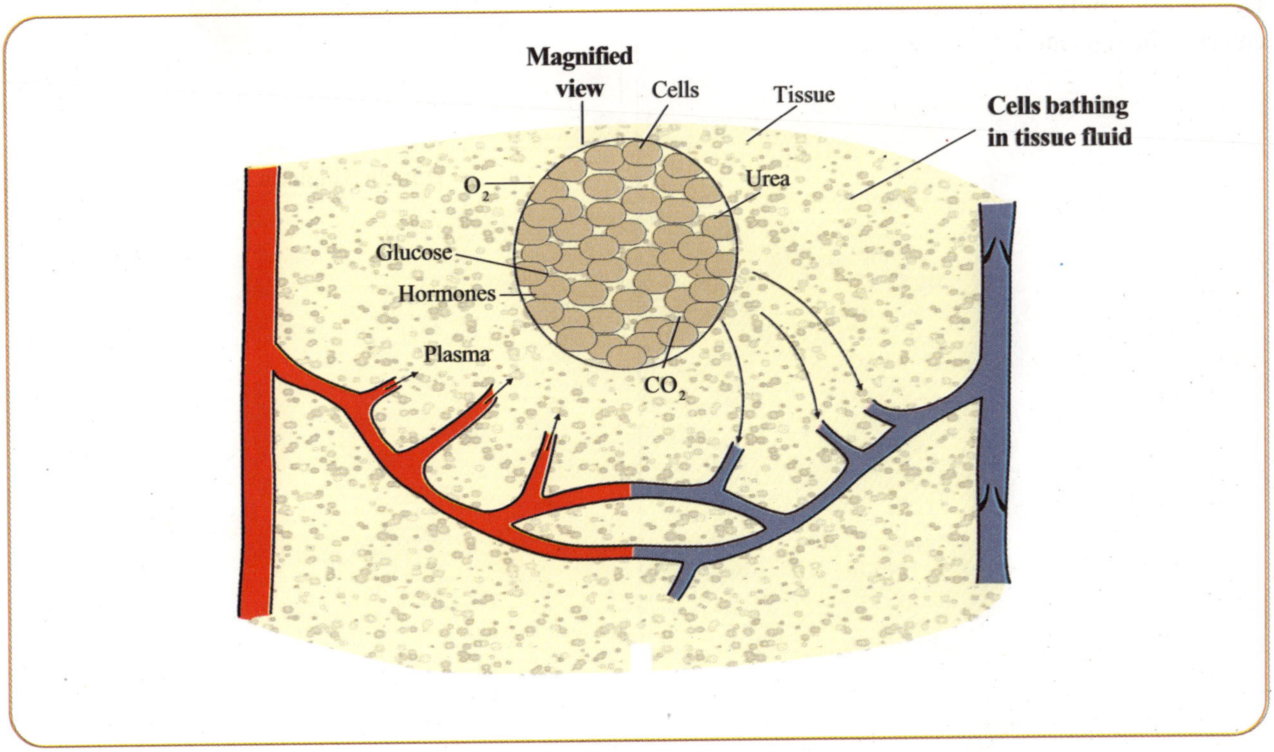

Exchange of materials at the cellular level

Lymphatic system

Some of the tissue fluid on its way back into capillaries enters the lymphatic system and flows as **lymph**. It is colourless and has all the elements of blood except red blood cells and platelets. The lymphatic system consists of lymphatic vessels, capillaries and lymph.

- Lymphatic system returns proteins and fluids to the bloodstream.
- It maintains the balance between the tissue fluid and blood.
- It also prevents infection.

Lymphatic vessels Thin walled, valves which are present ensure one-directional flow of lymph (from tissues to the heart).

Lymph nodes Small globular masses of lymphatic tissue, produce lymphocytes which engulf bacteria and prevent infection.

Lymphatic ducts Open into the pair of veins entering the right atria.

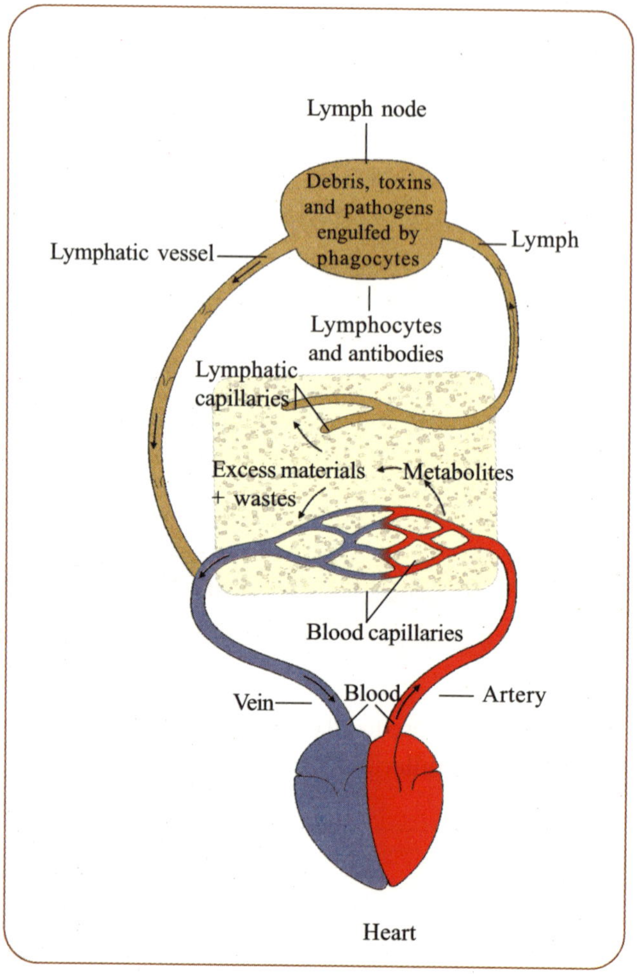

Human lymphatic system

EXERCISES

I. Very Short Answer Questions

(1 mark)

1. Name the tissue involved in the transportation of water and minerals in plants.
2. Name the substance mainly translocated in plants.
3. What are companion cells?
4. How water lost through transpiration is replenished?
5. What do you mean by the term 'transpiration'?
6. Which of the following is responsible for absorbing water in plants—stomata or root hair?
7. In which form is the organic food transported in plants?
8. Give the term used for transportation of food from leaves to different parts of the plant.
9. Name the two kinds of cells in xylem.
10. Which conducting tissue in plants is made up of mainly living cells?
11. Which among the two—plants or animals have a more efficient vascular system?
12. How does water flow from one tracheid to the next tracheid?
13. Name a plant which does not have a well developed transport system.
14. Name the system responsible for transportation of materials in the human body.
15. Where are RBCs formed?
16. What is the fluid component of blood called as?
17. Name the constituent of blood that helps in the transportation of oxygen in the human body.
18. What are leucocytes?
19. What is the average life span of RBCs?
20. Name one useful and one waste product transported by the blood.
21. What are lymphocytes?
22. How many times does the heart of a normal person beat per minute?
23. Name the protective covering of heart.
24. Which is the other term used for extracellular fluid?
25. Name the receiving chambers and pumping chambers of human heart.
26. Name the artery which contains deoxygenated blood.
27. Which of the two are thick walled—arteries or veins?
28. Why are capillaries thin walled?
29. What is the main function of lymphocytes?
30. What is the pulse rate of a normal human adult?
31. How is back flow of blood prevented in veins?
32. From where does the cardiac impulse originates?
33. What is oxygenated blood?
34. How transportation of minerals and water is carried in small plants?
35. How conduction of water and minerals in non-flowering plants is different from that in flowering plants?

36. What makes the walls of xylem water proof?
37. State the role played by transpiration other than upward movement of sap.
38. From where do the buds get energy to grow during spring season?
39. What makes red blood corpuscles red in colour?
40. Name a non-nucleated cell present in blood and state one of its most important function.
41. How can we measure the blood pressure?
42. Define tissue fluid.
43. At which phase of the cardiac cycle both atria and ventricles are relaxed simultaneously?
44. What is the role of blood pressure in circulation of blood?
45. What are antibodies?

II. Short Answer Questions

(2 marks)

1. What is the need of special tissues or organs for transport of substances in plants and animals?
2. What are the main differences between xylem and phloem?
3. Why is transportation of materials necessary in living organisms?
4. Write a short note on transportation of water and minerals in plants.
5. How is transpiration associated with absorption of water by roots?
6. What is translocation?
7. What will happen if xylem is removed from the plant?
8. 'Blood is a fluid connective tissue.' Justify.
9. Why are white blood corpuscles called 'soldiers' of the body?
10. How are red blood corpuscles different from white blood corpuscles?
11. Mention two ways in which blood protects the body against infection.
12. Why is clotting of blood an important phenomenon?
13. How is the composition of blood in pulmonary artery different from that in pulmonary vein?
14. Why are the walls of ventricles thinner than the walls of atria?
15. Why there is no mixing of oxygenated and deoxygenated blood in the human heart?
16. How is heartbeat different from pulse rate?
17. Why does the heart rate changes when the person starts exercising from normal resting state?
18. How is lymph different from blood?
19. Why lymph has less proteins than plasma?
20. What are the two main functions of lymph?
21. Why is SA node called pacemaker of heart?
22. Why is lymph called extracellular fluid?
23. Why the drugs or medicines are generally injected in a vein and not in artery?
24. How do lymph nodes prevent infection?
25. State two structural differences between an artery and a vein.
26. What can happen due to constriction of arterioles?

III. Short Answer Questions

(3 marks)

1. Write a short note on transportation of water and minerals in plants.
2. Differentiate between active transport and passive transport.

3. Explain the structure of tracheids and vessels.
4. How is water absorbed by the roots in plants?
5. What are the two kinds of xylem elements? How are they different from a blood vessel?
6. List the components of blood.
7. What do you understand by the term 'double circulation'? Why is there a need of double circulation in man?
8. What comprises the blood vascular system?
9. How are minerals taken up by plants?
10. How sugar molecules are transported to all parts of the plant body?
11. What would be the consequences of the deficiency of haemoglobin in blood of man?
12. 'Arteries carry blood at high pressure.' Justify.
13. Why is it necessary to separate oxygenated and deoxygenated blood in birds and mammals?

IV. Long Answer Questions

(5 marks)

1. Justify transpiration as a factor promoting ascent of sap.
2. Describe the vascular system involved in transportation of water and minerals in plants.
3. Discuss the structure and function of tissues responsible for the process of translocation in plants.
4. Draw a well labelled diagram showing movement of water molecules from root hairs to xylem.
5. What is blood? Describe its composition.
6. Discuss the functions of blood.
7. Briefly discuss the various types of blood vessels found in man.
8. Explain the structure of heart with the help of a well labelled diagram.
9. Give the schematic representation of the path taken by blood in man. Explain double circulation.
10. What is a cardiac cycle? Explain the changes in heart during one cardiac cycle.
11. Explain the features of human lymphatic system.
12. Give reasons.
    (a) The blood does not clot inside the undamaged blood vessels.
    (b) Donating blood is not at all harmful to the body.
13. Draw a diagram showing blood in the capillaries exchanging materials with cells of the tissues.
14. Discuss the there important function of lymphatic system.
15. Describe how oxygenated blood from the concerned chamber of heart is received and distributed to all parts of the body.
16. Trace the path of deoxygenated blood from the concerned chamber of heart.

TEST YOURSELF

Fill in the blanks

1. ______ transports water and ______ transports food in a plant.
2. The movement of water in plants takes the following path:
   Epidermis of root hair ______ ______ ______.
3. The upward movement of water is called ______.
4. Food is transported as ______ in plants.

5. ______ is an oxygen carrying pigment in the red blood corpuscles of man.
6. Cardiac impulse orginates from ______ in the heart.
7. The blood brought by pulmonary veins into the heart is rich in ______.
8. ______ is the outer covering of heart.
9. ______ and ______ corpuscles constitute the lymph.
10. The normal pulse rate of a person is ______.
11. The average life of an RBC is ______ days.
12. The circulation of blood from heart to different organs and back to heart is called ______.

Multiple-Choice Questions

Choose the correct option.

1. Inside the plant body water is transported through
   (a) cortex (b) root hair
   (c) xylem (d) phloem

2. Ascent of sap occurs mainly due to
   (a) root pressure (b) transpiration
   (c) osmosis (d) capillary action

3. Translocation of food occurs in the form of
   (a) starch (b) cellulose
   (c) sucrose (d) glucose

4. Which is not the function of blood?
   (a) regulation of body temperature
   (b) protection against infection
   (c) transport of oxygen
   (d) oxidation of food

5. Translocation of food is an
   (a) active process
   (b) passive process
   (c) semiactive process
   (d) none of these

6. Major part of the plasma consists of
   (a) blood cells (b) organic substances
   (c) minerals (d) water

7. Which of the following is not associated with clotting of blood?
   (a) fibrin (b) bilirubin
   (c) calcium (d) vitamin K

8. Contraction of right ventricle pumps blood into
   (a) right auricle (b) pulmonary artery
   (c) pulmonary vein (d) dorsal aorta

9. The WBCs destroys the foreign body by one of the following process
   (a) pinocytosis (b) digestion
   (c) phagocytosis (d) none of these

10. ____ helps the clot to form
    (a) pus (b) plasma
    (c) serum (d) platelets

11. Which of the following blood vessels is the thinnest of all?
    (a) lymph vessel (b) capillary
    (c) artery (d) vein

12. Lymphocytes present in lymph help in
    (a) carrying O_2 (b) carrying CO_2
    (c) fighting infection (d) blood clotting

13. During atrial contraction
    (a) deoxygenated blood from right atrium goes to right ventricle
    (b) oxygenated blood from right atrium goes to right ventricle
    (c) deoxygenated blood from left atrium goes to left ventricle

(d) deoxygenated blood from right ventricle goes to pulmonary vein

14. The main blood vessel that brings deoxygenated blood to heart is
    (a) aorta
    (b) vena cava
    (c) coronary blood vessel
    (d) pulmonary artery

15. The main blood vessel that distributes oxygenated blood to all parts is
    (a) aorta (b) pulmonary vein
    (c) vena cava (d) pulmonary artery

16. Phloem is responsible for transportation of
    (a) sucrose (b) hormones
    (c) amino acids (d) all of the above

17. In a systole
    (a) ventricles relax and take in blood from the atria
    (b) ventricles contract and force blood into arteries
    (c) atria contract and force blood into ventricles
    (d) both atria and ventricles are in relaxed state

18. In fishes
    (a) blood is pumped to gills for oxygenation
    (b) blood is pumped to heart for oxygenation
    (c) gills play no role in oxygenation
    (d) none of the above is applicable

Answers to Multiple-Choice Questions

1. (c)	2. (b)	3. (c)	4. (d)
5. (a)	6. (d)	7. (b)	8. (c)
9. (c)	10. (d)	11. (b)	12. (c)
13. (a)	14. (b)	15. (a)	16. (d)
17. (b)	18. (a)		

4 EXCRETION

The removal of excess, waste or harmful materials resulting from the biochemical reactions that occur within the cells of living organisms is known as **excretion**. During these reactions, water content in the body of an organism may increase or decrease.

Excretion in animals

- Different organisms have different method of excretion.
- **Protozoans,** the unicellular organisms, have no organ of excretion.
  - The waste product is diffused out from the general body surface.
- In flatworms, **flame cells** are the excretory organs.
- The earthworm has excretory tubules (called **nephridia**) in the body which extract waste matter from the body and discharge it either in the alimentary canal or outside through the pores.
- **Molluscs** have **kidney**, located near the heart as an excretory organ.
- Humans also have **kidneys** as the excretory organs.
- The excretory organs have evolved with the evolution of mulicellular complex organisms.

Excretion in humans

In human beings kidney is the main organ of excretion. Apart from it the skin, lungs and liver also serve the function of excretion.

Skin Sweat consists of water, salts and traces of urea. These substances are expelled (or excreted) from the body on sweating. However, sweating is a response to a rise in temperature and does not bring about a change in the blood composition.

Liver The bile pigments (formed due to breakdown of old RBC in the liver) and toxins are removed by liver.

Lungs They excrete carbon dioxide and water vapour produced during respiration.

The concept map on page 51 refers to the checklist of points given below.

Checklist for excretion in human beings

- The main excretory waste is nitrogeneous in nature which is urea/or uric acid. It is removed from the blood in the kidney.

1 ◆ The excretory system of humans consists of kidneys, ureters, urinary bladder and urethra.

- The **kidneys** are the main organs of excretion. They are bean shaped, two in number located in the abdomen.

- The **ureter** is a long tube. Two ureters one from each kidney open in the urinary bladder.
- The **urinary bladder** is pear shaped. The urine collects in the bladder.
- The **urethra** is a muscular tube starting from the bladder and opens to the exterior.

2 ◆ Each kidney consists of about one million tiny tubules called **nephrons**.

- The nephron is the working unit of a kidney. It is responsible for the excretion of urea and other wastes from the body.
- Each nephron has a cup-shaped upper end, called **Bowman's capsule**.
- The horseshoe-shaped Bowman's capsule surrounds a knot of blood capillaries called the **glomerulus**. These capillaries arise from renal artery, which brings wastes and excess water to kidneys.

3 ◆ The process of excretion is divided into three stages—filtration, selective reabsorption and tubular secretion.

- **Filtration** The waste material along with blood is brought to kidneys by the renal arteries.
  - Blood reaching the glomerulus is under high pressure which forces **(ultrafiltration)** waste materials, glucose, salts and other materials in solution through the walls of the capillaries into the Bowman's capsule.
  - The substances in solution form the **glomerular filtrate**.
- **Selective reabsorption** As the filtrate travels through the tubular parts of nephron, glucose, aminoacids, salts and other useful substances are absorbed. The useful substances are brought back into the blood by blood capillaries surrounding the nephron.
  - At the end of its journey, the filtrate is called **urine**. Its composition is different because of the reabsorption of useful substances since it started out in the Bowman's capsule.
- **Tubular secretion** The nephrons drain the urine into kidney through **collecting ducts** leading to ureter. From ureter it reaches urinary bladder which is muscular and under nervous control where it is stored till thrown out of the body.

Questions

1. Where do kidneys lie in the human body? (1 mark)
2. Apart from kidney, list other organs that serve the function of excretion. (2 marks)

Kidney failure and dialysis

The kidney of a person may fail due to some infection, injury and extremes of blood pressure.

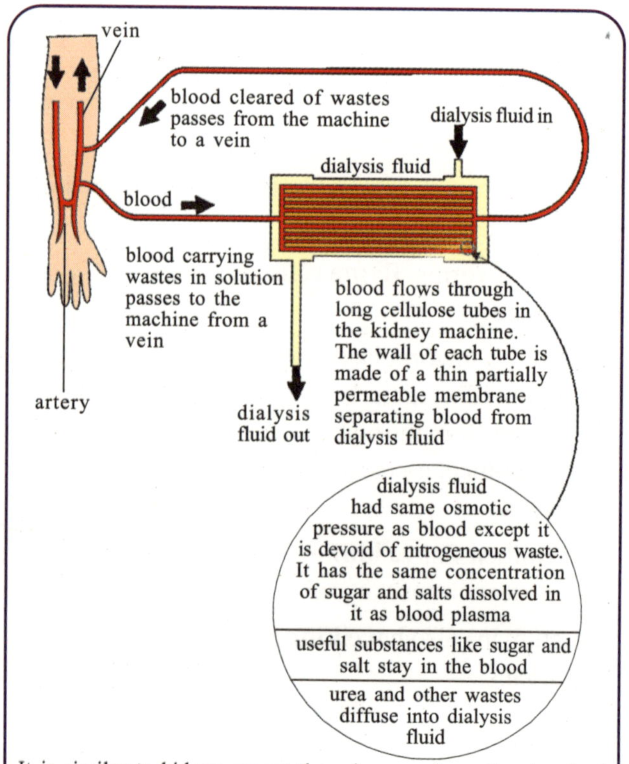

It is similar to kidney except there is no reabsorption involved. Normally, in an healthy adult, initial filtrate in kidney is 180 litres daily. However volume actually excreted is only a litre or two a day because the remaining filtrate is reabsorbed by the kidney tubules.

How a kidney machine works

THE HUMAN EXCRETORY SYSTEM

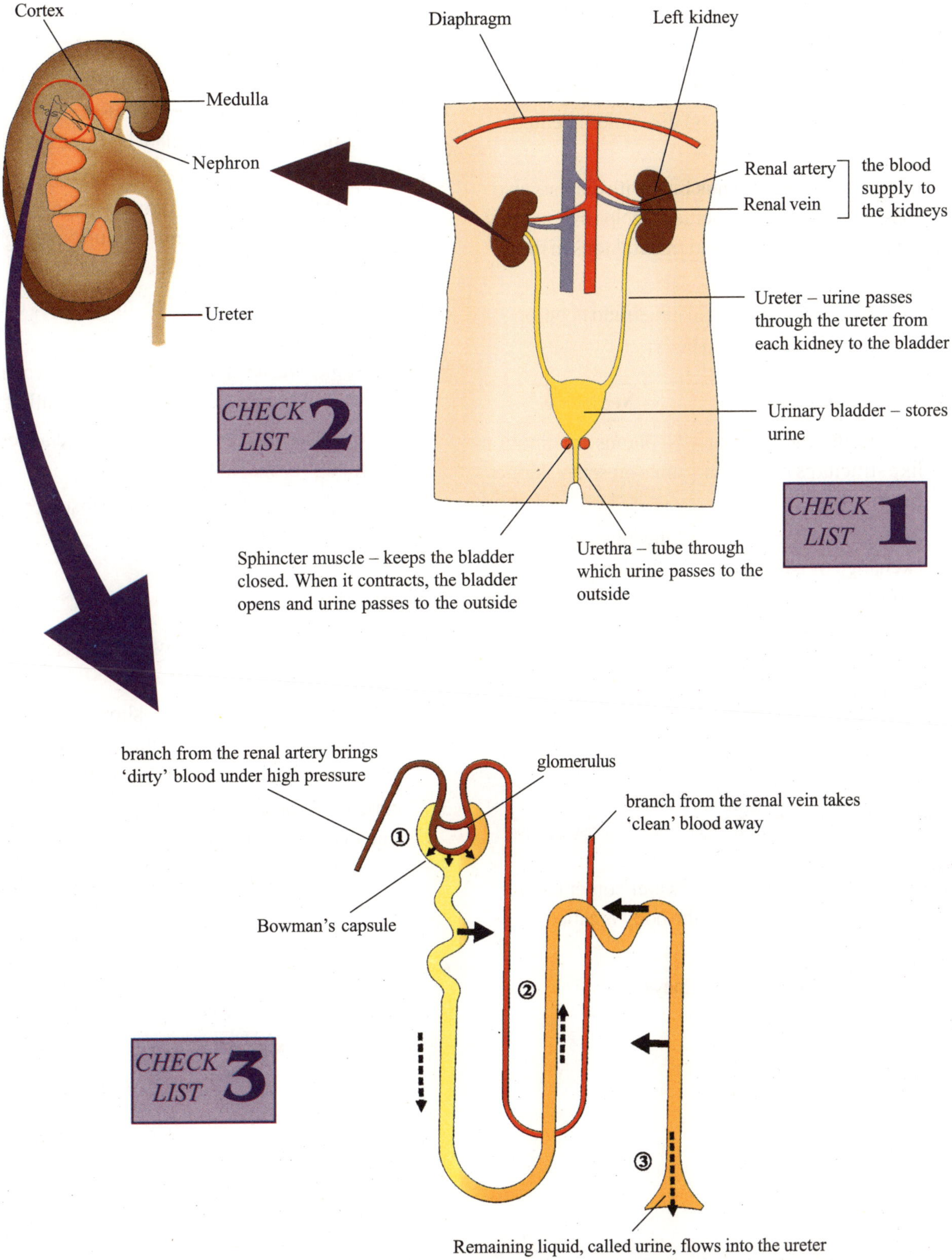

If a person's kidneys are not working (kidney failure) then:

- poisonous urea accumulates in the blood.
- water accumulates in the tissues of the body.

  As a result, the person dies unless treated quickly.

Use of artificial kidney (a machine with dialysis also called as hemodialysis membranes) helps maintaining the normal levels of water and mineral ions in the body fluids.

◆ Comparison of alveoli (in lungs) and nephron (in kidneys) of a human body.

Alveoli	Nephrons
1. Alveoli are small balloon like structures present in lungs.	Nephrons are filtration units present in kidney.
2. Provide a surface for exchange of gases in respiration.	Filter blood in excretion.
3. The walls contain an extensive network of blood vessels.	It has a capillary cluster—glomerulus.

Osmoregulation

◆ The process of control of water content and concentration of ions in the body is called **osmoregulation**.

◆ It is brought about by Kidneys.

Excretion in Plants

Excretion in plants is different from that in animals as the physilogy is different. The various waste products and their elimination from the plant body are as follows:

- Excess gases whether oxygen released during photosynthesis or carbon dioxide given out in respiration are released into the surroundings through stomata.
- Excess water is given out by the process of transpiration.
- Metabolic wastes may be stored in cell vacuoles or they can accumulate in leaves that fall off.
- Some other waste products are stored as resins and gums in old xylem.
- Plants also excrete some waste substances into the soil.

Questions

1. How do kidneys conserve water and useful molecules? (3 marks)
2. With the help of a flow chart, show the process of removal of waste from a human body. (2 marks)
3. Name the substances that are reabsorbed as the urine flows along the tube. (2 marks)
4. On what factors does the amount of water to be re-absorbed during excretion depends on? (2 marks)
5. List two vital functions of kidney. (2 marks)
6. What is osmoregulation? (1 mark)
7. How artificial kidney helps in excretion? (2 marks)

EXERCISES

I. Very Short Answer Questions

(1 mark)

1. Define excretion.
2. Which cell organelle acts as an excretory unit in *Amoeba?*
3. Name the basic nitrogenous waste products of metabolism.
4. Name the structural and functional unit of kidney.
5. Which artery branches to form glomerulus?
6. What happens to glucose which enters the nephron along with the filtrate?
7. Where is urine stored in the body?
8. Name the tube that connects kidneys to the urinary bladder.
9. Name the chief nitrogenous waste product present in urine.
10. What is urethra?
11. Name the network of capillaries present in the cup-like Bowman's capsule.
12. Name the part of nephron in which glomerulus is enclosed.
13. Which blood vessel carries dirty blood into the kidneys?
14. What happens to the useful substances which flow into nephron along with the waste material?
15. What is glomerular filtrate?
16. Where is urine carried through ureters?
17. What is the function of kidney other than removing toxic wastes from the body?
18. What can be done to save a patient with kidney failure?
19. What is produced as a result of biochemical reactions occurring in a cell?
20. How is excretion carried out in protozoans?
21. Name the phenomenon by which *Amoeba* excretes its waste.
22. Why bile pigments are formed?
23. Which part of kidney acts as dialysis bag?
24. What is the role of sphincter muscle?
25. Name the procedure used in the working of artificial kidney.
26. Name two sections of kidney.
27. What is dialysis fluid?
28. Which part of nephron is located in cortex of kidney?

II. Short Answer Questions

(2 marks)

1. Name the different parts of a nephron.
2. List the three steps involved in urine formation.
3. State two vital functions of human kidney.
4. How do kidneys conserve water when its contents are low in the body?
5. Why nephron has a long tubule?
6. Why blood reaching the glomerulus is under high pressure?
7. What do you mean by selective reabsorption?

8. Why the tubules of nephron have a rich supply of blood vessels?
9. What is the composition of urine?
10. Why is excretion important for an organism?
11. Trace the path of urine from kidney to outside in man.
12. Differentiate between ureter and urethra.
13. What is dialysis?
14. What happens in case of kidney failure and malfunctioning?
15. In a dialysis machine, the tubes are made up of which substance? What does the dialysis solution contains?
16. How is excretion carried out in earthworm?
17. Explain how skin performs the role of excretion. What other important functioning is controlled due to sweating?
18. List the reasons of kidney failure.
19. How dialysis fluid is different from blood?
20. Though kidney filters 180 litres daily, the volume of urine excreted is a litre or two. Why?

III. Long Answer Questions

(5 marks)

1. Which is the major nitrogenous waste product in human beings? How is it removed from the body?
2. Describe the three steps involved in urine formation.
3. Draw a well labelled diagram of human excretory system.
4. Describe the structure of kidney and discuss its function.
5. Explain how artificial kidney carries out the function of cleaning blood.
6. What is a nephron? Describe its structure with the help of a diagram.
7. Draw a well labelled diagram showing how kidney machine works.
8. Discuss the different ways by which plants eliminate their wastes.
9. How hemodialysis is different from the functioning of kidney?

TEST YOURSELF

Fill in the blanks

1. *Amoeba* removes excretory wastes and excess of water from its body by ______.
2. Waste products are formed as a result of ______ in the body.
3. Filtration of blood in the kidney occurs in ______.
4. The forcing of wastes, glucose, etc. through the walls of the capillaries into Bowman's capsule is called ______.
5. ______ constitute the excretory system in flatworms.
6. A reservoir where urine is collected is called ______.
7. Artificial kidney works on the principle of ______.

Multiple-Choice Questions

Choose the correct option.

1. Which is applicable to human kidney?
   (a) It is located near heart.
   (b) It is bean shaped.

(c) It has several nephridia.
(d) Each kidney has two ureters.

2. The human urine mainly contains
(a) urea (b) uric acid
(c) ammonia (d) CO_2

3. The vital morphological and physiological units of a human kidney are
(a) nephridia (b) seminiferous tubules
(c) ureters (d) nephron

4. Which of the following is completely reabsorbed from glomerular filtrate in the nephron?
(a) urea (b) salts
(c) glucose (d) uric acid

5. Artificial removal of metabolic wastes from the body is known as
(a) ultrafiltration (b) dialysis
(c) diapedesis (d) osmoregulation

6. In nephron, glucose, amino acids and other useful products are reabsorbed into the blood by
(a) glomerulus (b) blood capillaries
(c) long tubule (d) Bowman's capsule

7. Encircle the odd one out
(a) skin (b) lung
(c) nephron (d) heart

8. Trace the correct path of urine formation
(a) Renal vein → Glomerulus → Tubular part → Collecting duct
(b) Renal artery → Glomerulus → Tubular part → Collecting duct
(c) Renal artery → Bowman's capsule → Glomerulus → Collecting duct
(d) Renal vein → Bowman's capsule → Glomerulus → Collecting duct

9. The process which is not involved in excretion in case of humans is
(a) filtration (b) selective absorption
(c) diffusion (d) tubular secretion

10. Kidneys do not help in
(a) maintaining normal levels of water
(b) maintaining mineral ions in the body fluid
(c) removing nitrogenous waste like urea
(d) removing worn out RBCs

Answers to Multiple-Choice Questions

1. (b)	2. (a)	3. (d)	4. (c)
5. (b)	6. (b)	7. (d)	8. (c)
9. (c)	10. (d)		

5 CONTROL AND COORDINATION

The ability of organisms to detect changes and make appropriate responses is essential for their survival. A **stimulus** is a change in the environment which causes a living organism to respond. The response to stimuli varies in different organisms. Stimuli may be certain environmental factors such as light, heat, cold and pressure.

Coordination in plants

Plants show two different types of movement—one dependent on growth and the other independent of growth.

Plants do not have any specialised cells or an elaborate control system for responding to stimuli. However, plants respond to stimuli such as light, touch and gravitational force. Both external and internal factors regulate growth and movements in plants. In plants the information is transmitted in the form of electrical and chemical impulses. Since there is no specialised tissue to conduct the impulses, it is done by the change in the shapes of cells. A plant cell shrinks or swells to bring about the change in its shape.

Response to stimulus

There are responses or movements that are neither towards nor away from the stimulus. For example, flowers open and close in response to changes in temperature. Also the leaves of plant 'touch-me-not' (*Mimosa pudica*) bend and droop on touching. *Mimosa* shows rapid movement which is uncommon in plants. Stomatal movement observed in plants is due to the change in amount of water in the cell. This also results in swelling or shrinking and therefore the change in shapes of the cells.

Movement due to growth

Tropic or directional movements (tropisms) are responses or movement of a plant in the direction of stimuli or away from it. For example, shoots bend towards light. The stem grows away from the pull of gravity.

Activity 1

1. Taken an empty jam bottle and fill it with water.
2. Cover its mouth with a wire mesh and place two or three freshly germinated pea or gram seeds on it.
3. Take an empty cardboard box (you may use a shoe box) and keep it in a room in such a manner that its open side faces light coming from a window.
4. Observe after two or three days. You will find that shoots grow towards light and roots grow away from light.

5. Now turn the bottle so that shoot is away from light and root is towards light.
6. Observe after few days. You will see that the shoot and root have changed direction.

Response of the plant of the direction of light

Know about plant responses

1 ◆ Tropisms are positive if the plant grows towards the stimulus and negative if it grows away from it.

As a result of different positive and negative tropisms, the different parts of the plant grow in such a way that its chances of survival are increased.

2 ◆ Tropic movements are of various types depending upon the kind of stimuli.

- **Phototropism** means that when a growing plant is illuminated by unidirectional light, it responds by bending towards the light.
- Positive phototropism means that the shoot will always grow upwards.
- **Geotropism** means the downward movement of roots of plants in response to gravitational force.

  Positive geotropism means that the roots will always grow downwards.
- **Thigmotropism** is the response of stems of some types of plant to the touch of an object.

  The plant responds by growing tendrils that are sensitive ro touch. For example, sweet peas and runner beans climb up a support by means of tendrils.
- **Chemotropism** is the response due to chemical stimulus. For example, growth of the pollen tube towards ovules in response to chemical stimulus.
- **Hydrotropism** is the response of plants to the availability of water.

3 ◆ **Phytohormones** or plant growth regulators are chemical substances which perform the function of control and coordination. They are of different types. They are synthesised at places away from where they act and diffuse to areas of action.

◆ The hormones in plants control their directional growth.

◆ The synthesis and action of phytohormones are largely influenced by the external stimuli. For example, duration of light (the external stimulus) regulates flowering and seed germination in plants.

◆ Types of phytohormones include auxins, gibberellins, cytokinins, and abscisic acid.

- **Auxins** helps the cells to grow longer. Auxin diffuses and gets concentrated towards the shady side of the stem. Cells in this part of the stem grow longer so that the plant appears to bend towards light.
- **Gibberellins** helps in the growth of stem.
- **Cytokinins** are mainly present in fruits and seeds. They promote cell division.
- **Abscisic acid** inhibits growth and causes wilting of leaves, and fall of leaves and fruits.

Questions

1. How is the movement of leaves of the sensitive plant different from the movement of a shoot towards light? (2 marks)

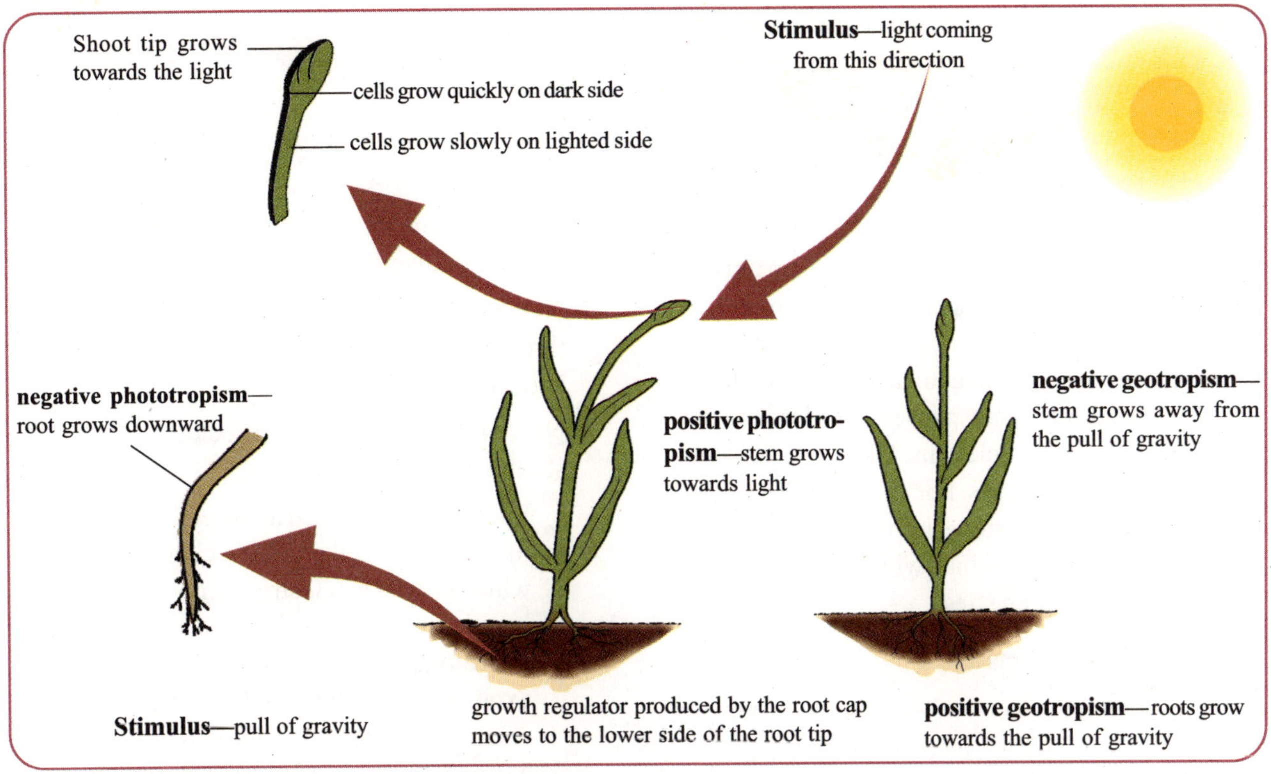

Tropisms—the response of the shoot tip to light and of the root cap to gravity and water.

2. Design an experiment to demonstrate hydrotropism. (5 marks)
3. Give an example of a plant hormone that promotes growth. (1 mark)

Coordination in animals

1 ◆ Unicellular animals and smaller multicellular animals do not have any specialised cells for perception of external stimuli.

2 ◆ Large multicellular animals have specialised cells called **neurons** or **nerve cells**, for responding to stimuli.

3 ◆ In multicellular animals such as mammals, the detection and response to external environmental changes, and the regulation of the internal environment of the body, are brought about by two systems—the **nervous system** and the **endocrine** or **hormonal system**. The two systems coordinate with each other.

Receptors Animals receive a variety of external information through specialised structures called **sense organs** or **receptors**. They are of different types on the basis of their specific functions.

- **Photoreceptors** for light.
- **Phonoreceptors** for sound.
- **Olfactoreceptors** or **chemoreceptors** for smell.
- **Gustatoryreceptors** for taste.
- **Thermoreceptors** for temperature.

◆ Sensory receptor cells detect stimuli and convert them into nerve impulses that transmit information, to which the body can respond.

◆ The brain is a centre for analysis of information related to hearing, vision, smell, taste, movement and other muscular actions.

- Neurons (nerve cells) that pass information from the receptors to the brain are **sensory**.
- The neurons that conduct nerve impulses from the brain to effectors like muscles or glands are **motor**.
- Muscles respond to nerve impulses by contracting. This is only possible when muscle cells change their shape. The special proteins present in the muscle cells undergo a change in their shape and arrangement in response to nervous electrical responses. This leads to the shortening of muscle cells. Glands respond by secreting substances. For example, the adrenal glands respond to nerve impulses by producing the hormone adrenaline, which helps the body to cope with sudden stress.

The whole process runs as

stimulus → receptor → nerves → effector → response

Human nervous system

The nervous system in humans is divided into central, peripheral and autonomic nervous systems.

- Nervous system receives stimulus (external or internal), processes and interprets it, and then responds accordingly.
  - The nervous system also passes information from one internal system to another.

    As a result nervous system controls and coordinates various functions in the body.
- The **central nervous system** comprises brain, and spinal cord. It receives information from all parts of the body and integrates it.

The numbers on the concept map on page 62–63 refer to the checklist of points below.

Checklist for the nervous system

1 ◆ Each **nerve** of the nervous system consists of a bundle of **neurons**.

- Neurons transmit nerve impulses to an effector (muscle or gland).
- **Nerve impulse** is the information passing through neurons in the form of minute electrical and chemical disturbances.
- Nerve impulses stimulate effectors to respond to stimuli in a useful way.
  - Information acquired at the end of dendritic tip of a nerve cell sets off a chemical reaction which creates an electrical impulse. This impulse travels from dendrite to cell body and then along the axon to its end. At the end of axon, the electrical impulse releases some chemicals which cross the synapse and start a similar electrical impulse in the dendrite of next neuron.
- A nerve impulse takes just milliseconds to travel along a neuron.

2 ◆ Neuron is the functional and structural unit of nervous system and the largest cell found in the human body. A neuron has three components:

  - **cell body**—like a typical cell containing nucleus and granular cytoplasm. It sends of the electrical impulses to axon.
  - **dendrites**—thin extensions of the cell body that carry nerve impulses to the cell body. They acquire information.
  - **axon**—single long thin extension of the cell body that carries nerve impulses from the cell body as electrical impulses.
- **Synapses** are the functional junctions between neurons. In other words, they are minute gaps that separate neurons from one another.
  - Any information acquired at the transmission of the nerve cell is transmitted in the form of an electrical impulse.

- This impulse travels along the axon to its end where it induces the release of some chemicals. The chemicals then cross the gap or synapse and start a similar electrical impulse in the adjacent neuron.
- A similar synapse further allows the transmission of nerve impulse.
- Thus, synapse helps converting electrical impulse into chemical impulse during its transmission.

3 ◆ The highly developed central nervous system in human beings consists of brain and spinal cord.

◆ **Brain** is the highest coordinating system in the body. It is protected by a bony box called **cranium** in the skull.

◆ Brain is covered by three membranes called **meninges**.

- **Cerebrospinal fluid** is filled in space between membranes to protect the brain from mechanical shocks.

◆ The brain is broadly divided into three parts— forebrain, midbrain and hindbrain.

◆ The forebrain is the main thinking part of the brain and consists of cerebrum and olfactory lobes.

- The **cerebrum** is the largest, most complex and specialised part of the brain. It controls voluntary actions.
- It has sensory areas where information (impulse) is received. Also there is motor area from where impulses are sent to muscle or effector organs.
- There are specific regions for each kind of stimulus and its response in the cerebrum. For example, for visual reception, auditory reception, touch, smell, temperature and conscious association and muscular activities.

◆ Midbrain and hindbrain control all involuntary actions.

- The midbrain includes regions which are the centres of vision.
- The hindbrain consists of cerebellum, pons and medulla oblongata. Generally, it controls all involuntary actions.
- The **cerebellum** controls balance and the action of muscles which makes precise and coordinated movement possible.
- The **pons** takes part in regulation of respiration.
- The **medulla oblongata** controls involuntary actions. It is the regulating centre for swallowing, coughing, sneezing, vomiting and blood pressure.

4 ◆ **Spinal cord** is cylindrical and arises from the medulla oblongata and runs all along the vertebral column.

◆ The spinal cord is the centre of reflex action, and the sensory and motor nerves constitute the reflex arc.

◆ **Reflex responses** happen before the brain has had time to process the nerve impulses carrying the information about the stimulus. For example, we suddenly withdraw our hands or legs on getting the prick of a pin, or touching a very hot or cold substance. This type of involuntary motor response to a stimulus is called a **reflex action**. Knee-jerk reflex is another example of reflex action. While sitting with freely hanging legs, a sudden strike below the knee cap kicks the leg forward. Coughing, blinking of eyes, yawning, sneezing and movement of the diaphragm are also reflex actions.

- Nerves from all over the body meet in a bundle in the spinal cord on their way to brain.
- A reflex arc is formed in the spinal cord but the information is passed on to the brain also.
- A **reflex arc** is the chain of nerves entering, within and leaving the nerve cord, along which nerve impulses travel to bring about a reflex response. Each nerve is represented by one neuron.

THE HUMAN NERVOUS SYSTEM

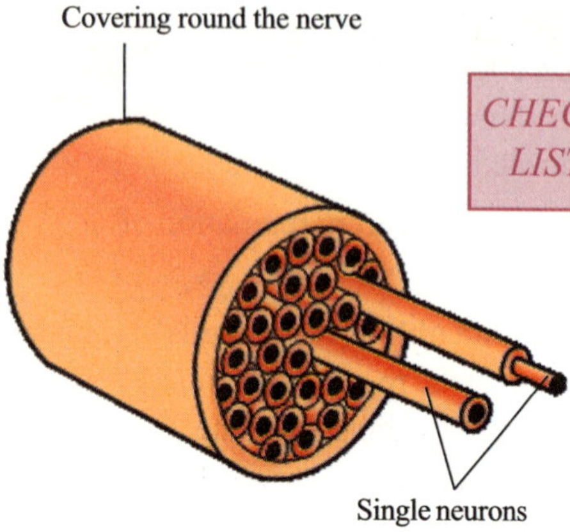

Bundle of neurons forming nerve

CHECK LIST 1

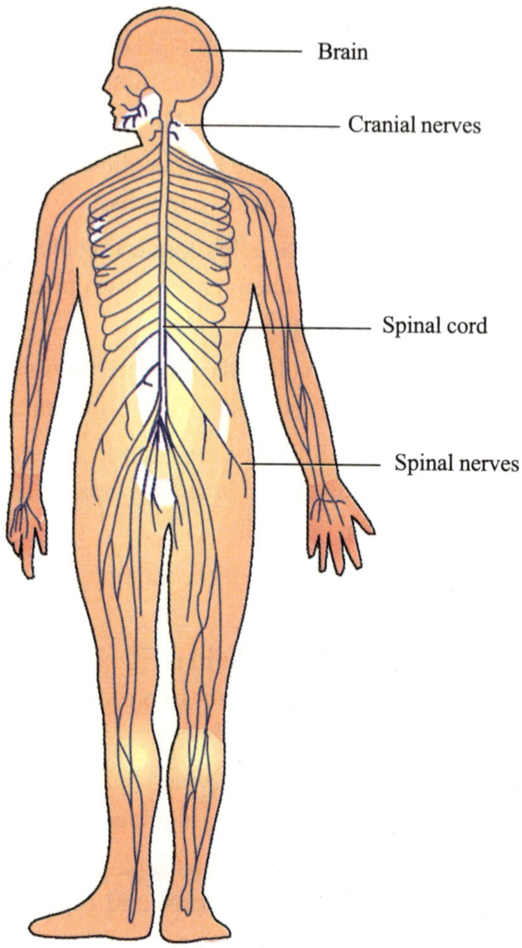

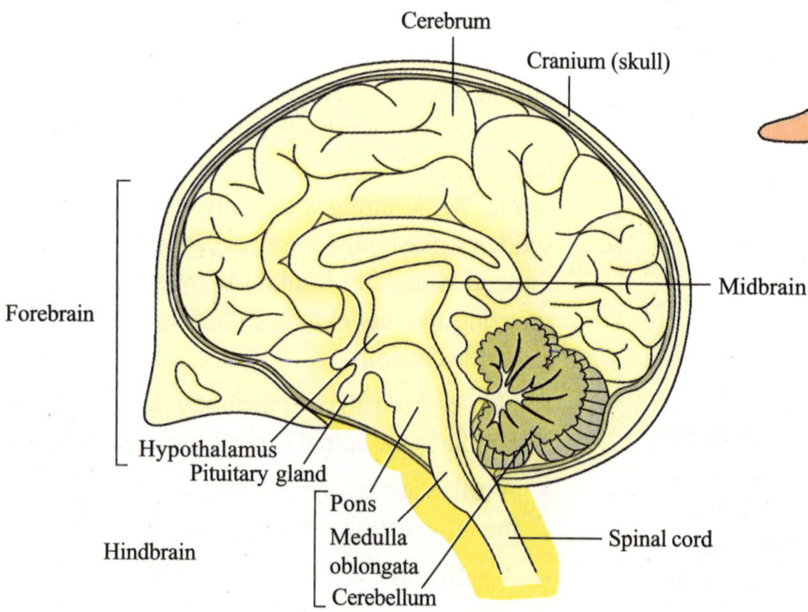

Human brain

CHECK LIST 3

Nerve cell or neuron

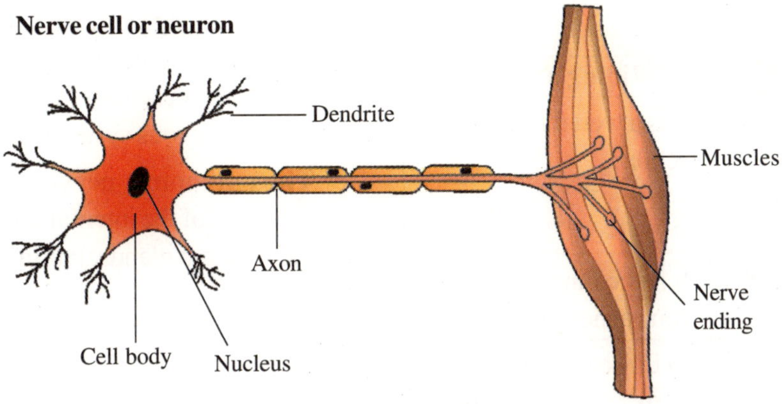

CHECK LIST 2

The reflex arc

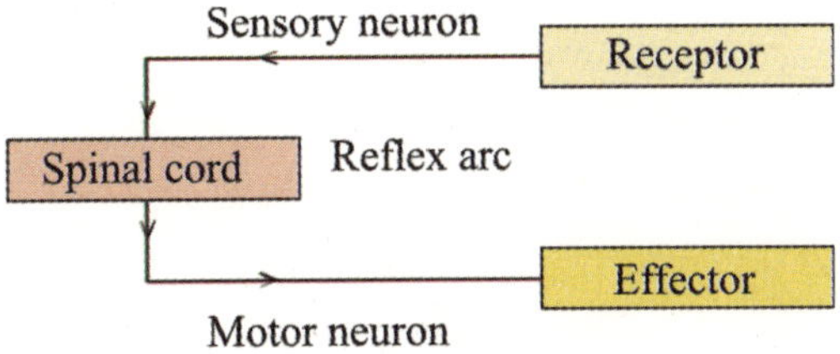

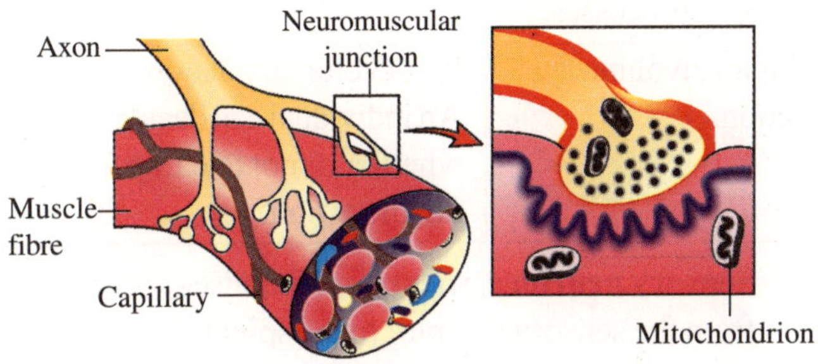

Neuromuscular junction

CHECK LIST 4

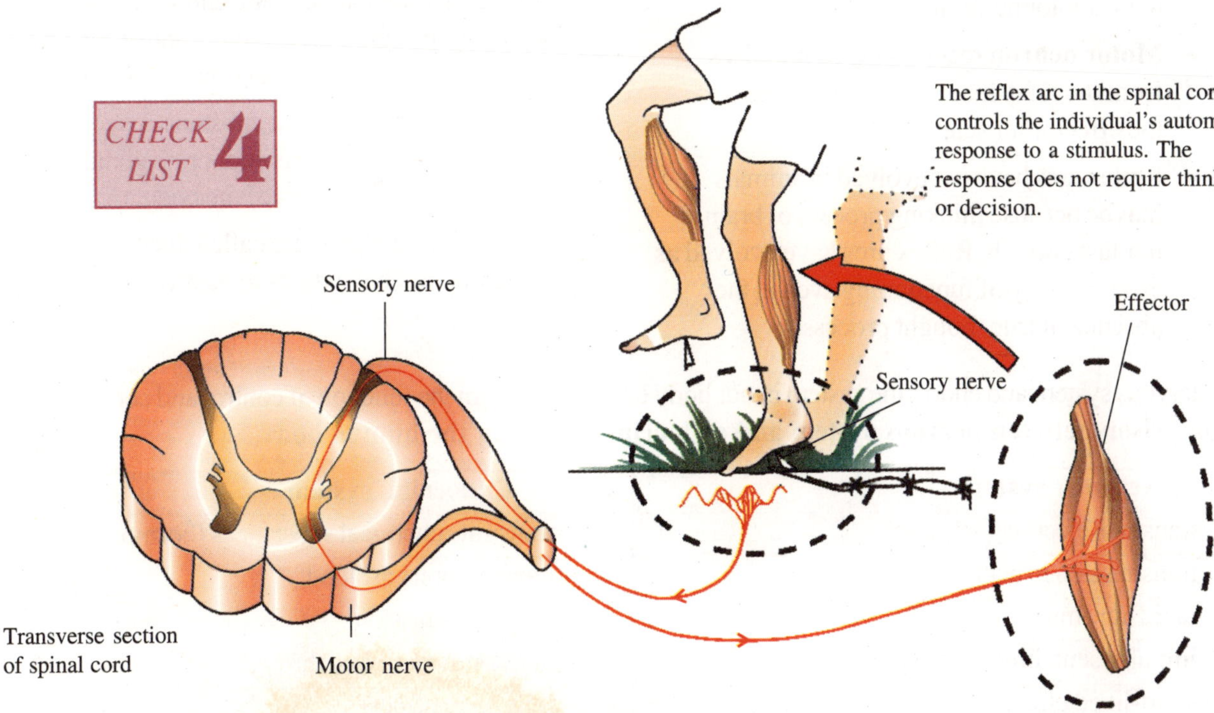

The reflex arc in the spinal cord controls the individual's automatic response to a stimulus. The response does not require thinking or decision.

Differences between reflex action and riding a bicycle.

Reflex action	Riding a bicycle
a. Reflex action is a sudden action in response to a change in the environmental.	It is a well thought of action.
b. It is the function of spinal cord.	It is the function of the central nervous system.
c. Reflex arc works efficiently in the absence of the thought processes.	In this case the brain thinks and takes actions based on that thinking.
d. It is an involuntary action.	It is a voluntary action. An individual can decide whether or not to carry out the action.

- **Sensory neuron** carries nerve impulses from the sensory receptor to the spinal cord.
- **Relay neuron** receives nerve impulses from the sensory neuron and passes them to the motor neutron.
- **Motor neuron** receives nerve impulses from the relay neuron and passes them to the effector muscle.
- Reflex arcs have not evolved in animals maybe because thinking process of brain is not fast enough. Reflex arcs have evolved as efficient way of functioning even in the absence of true thought process.

- **The peripheral nervous system** consists of nerves arising from the brain and the spinal cord known as cranial and spinal nerves respectively. Peripheral nervous system communicates with central nervous system.
- **The autonomic nervous system** controls the activities of the internal organs like, heart, lungs, kidneys and glands. It is involuntory in action.

Questions

1. What is the differences between a reflex action and walking? (2 marks)
2. How do we detect the smell of an incense stick? (2 marks)
3. What is the role of the brain in reflex action? (1 mark)

Hormones

- Besides nervous system, the endocrine or hormonal system is involved in control and coordination of various functions in animals.
- **Hormones** are chemical substances secreted in trace amounts by various endocrine glands located in different parts of the body.
- The endocrine glands are called ductless glands as they do not have ducts to pass their hormones.

The nervous system and endocrine system in our body together perform the function of control and coordination.

Comparison between nervous system and endocrine system in the human body.

Nervous system	Endocrine system
transmits electrical impulses	transmits chemical substances (hormones)
transmission in nerves	transmission via blood
rapid transmission	slow transmission
impulse sent directly to the target organ	hormones dispersed throughout the body
short-lived effects	long term effects

- When the hormones reach certain organs they change the rate or kind of activity of the organ.
- The blood system is the link between a hormone and its target tissue. The sequence reads as follows:

endocrine gland —produces→ **hormone** —circulates→ **blood** —affects→ **target tissue**

- Unlike plants, hormones in animals do not cause directional growth. The hormones do help in coordinated growth. The functions of the important hormones are as follows:
  1. **trophic hormones**—regulation of the secretion from endocrine gland like adrenal, thyroid, testes and ovary.
  2. **prolactin**—regulates the function of mammary gland.
  3. **vasopressin**—regulation of water and electrolyte balance.
  4. **oxytocin**—stimulation of muscles during child birth and lactation.
- **Pituitary gland** producing many hormones including **growth hormones** which help in development of bones and muscles. Deficiency of this hormone in childhood causes dwarfism whereas the excess makes an individual extremely tall.
- **Thyroid gland** produces hormone **thyroxin** which is involved in the regulation of metabolism of carbohydrates, fats and proteins. Iodine is essential for the synthesis of thyroxin. (Therefore we should have iodised salt.) Deficiency of iodine causes goitre (swollen neck).
- **Pancreas** secrete insulin and glucagon. **Insulin** is responsible for lowering of blood glucose.
  - **glucagon** causes the increase of blood glucose. If sugar level in blood rises pancreas respond by producing insulin.
- **Testis** secretes **testosterone** which regulates male accessory sex organs and secondary sexual characters like moustache, beard and voice.
- **Ovary** secretes **oestrogen** which regulates female accessory sex organs and secondary sexual characters like mammary gland, hair pattern, voice, and maintenance of pregnancy.
- **Adrenal gland** secretes **adrenaline** which regulates blood pressure, heart rate, carbohydrate metabolism and mineral balance (prepares body for sudden action).

> ☞ **Remember** the characteristics of a hormone
>
> * specific chemical messengers, so act on specific tissue or target organ.
> * poured directly into the blood and carried by blood circulation.
> * regulate growth, metabolic activities and reproduction.
> * too much or too little of a hormone can cause a metabolic disorder.

- The endocrine glands that perform dual functions are
  (a) the pancreas
  (b) the ovary and testes.

Apart from the secretion of hormones, pancreas also secretes digestive enzymes whereas testes and ovary produce gametes (sperm and ova).

THE HUMAN ENDOCRINE SYSTEM

1. **growth hormones**—development of bones and muscles
2. **trophic hormones**—regulation of the secretion from endocrine gland like adrenal, thyroid, testes and ovary
3. **prolactin**—regulates the function of mammary gland
4. **vasopressin**—regulation of water and electrolyte balance
5. **oxytocin**—stimulation of muscles during child birth and lactation

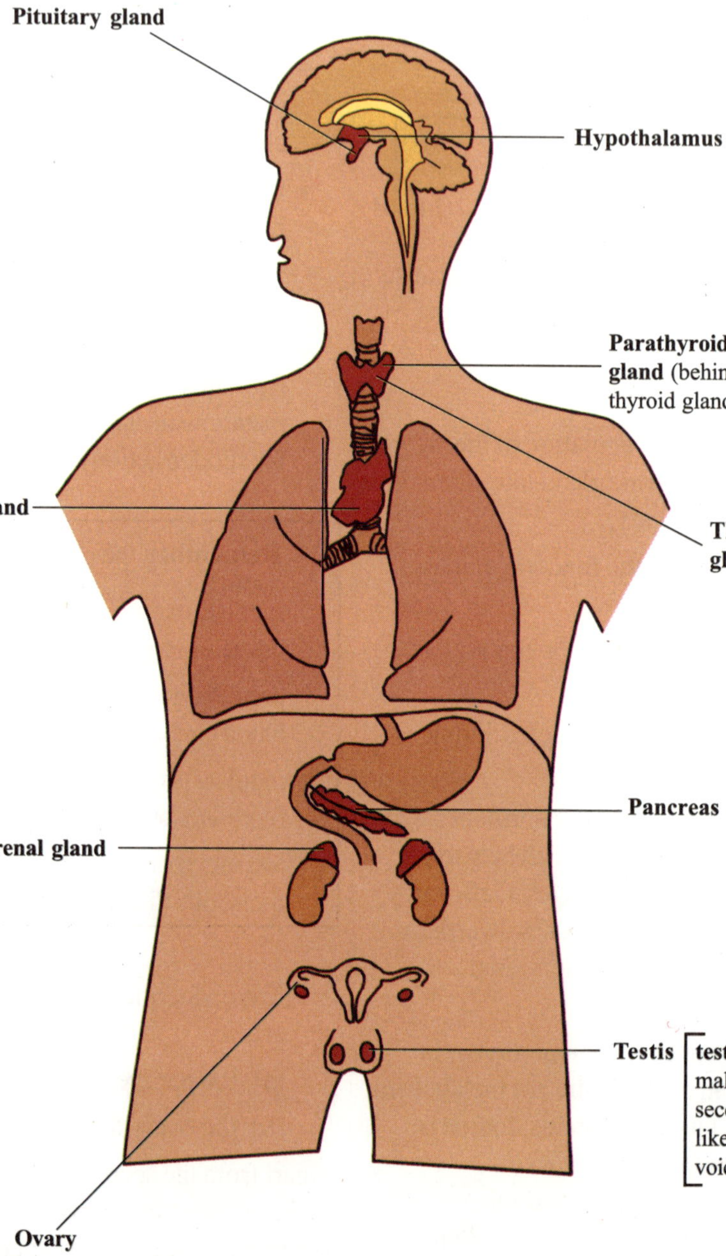

'releasing' and **'inhibiting' hormones**—regulation of the secretion of hormones from pituitary gland

calcitonin—regulation of blood calcium and phosphate

thymus hormone—plays role in development of immunity and formation of T cells

thyroxin—regulation of metabolism of carbohydrates, fats and proteins

1. **insulin**—lowering of blood glucose
2. **glucagon**—increase of blood glucose

1. **adrenaline** (from medulla)
2. **aldosterone** and **corticosterone** (from cortex)

regulation of blood pressure, heart rate, carbohydrate metabolism and mineral balance (prepares body for sudden action)

testosterone—regulation of male accessory sex organs and secondary sexual characters like moustache, beard and voice

oestrogen
progesterone
regulation of female accessory sex organs and secondary sexual characters like mammary gland, hair pattern and voice, maintenance of pregnancy

Note: The figure shows location of endocrine glands in different parts of the human body, the hormones secreted and their functions.

EXERCISES

I. Very Short Answer Questions

(1 mark)

1. Define stimuli.
2. What are phytohormones?
3. What is meant by tropism?
4. How does a growing plant respond when it is illuminated by unidirectional light?
5. What type of movement is shown by *Mimosa* plant when touched?
6. What is geotropism?
7. Name any four phytohormones found in plants.
8. Define phototropism.
9. Give one example of chemotropism.
10. Name the two main systems responsible for control and coordination in the human body.
11. What is the structural and functional unit of nervous system?
12. Define synapse.
13. What are the different types of nerves found in human body?
14. How many spinal nerves are present in man?
15. What is the function of a receptor?
16. Differentiate between dendrite and axon.
17. Which is the largest part of the brain?
18. Which endocrine gland is located in the brain?
19. List the hormones secreted by pituitary gland.
20. Name the hormone controlling lactation.
21. Which part of the brain is responsible to maintain equilibrium and posture of the body?
22. Name the gland which is exocrine as well as endocrine in nature.
23. Name the fluid which fills the cavities of the brain.
24. What is the function of the fluid that surrounds the human brain?
25. What is the significance of reflex arc?
26. How is a sensory nerve different from a motor nerve?
27. Which part of the brain is associated with intelligence?
28. Which part of the brain is concerned with muscular coordination?
29. How is spinal cord protected?
30. What do you understand by the term 'impulse'?
31. How does an impulse travel through a neuron?
32. What is the function of medulla oblongata?
33. Which is the control centre of the reflex action?
34. Why are endocrine glands called ductless?
35. What is cranium?
36. What are the two different types of movement shown by plants?
37. How can you differentiate between positive and negative tropisms?
38. Where is the analysis of information related to vision, smell, taste and hearing done?
39. Name the stress hormone.
40. Which part of the brain controls involuntary action?

41. Give one difference between plant hormone and animal hormone.
42. Which signals will get disrupted in case of a spinal cord injury?
43. Name the hormone which causes wilting in plants.
44. State one example of reflex action performed in our daily life.
45. Mention the source gland of thyroxine.

II. Short Answer Questions

(2 marks)

1. How does control and coordination takes place in plants?
2. Differentiate between phototropism and photoperiodism.
3. Classify the following as tropic or nastic movements:
   (a) roots moving downward
   (b) shoots bending towards light
   (c) plant growing in spiral around the object
   (d) opening of a flower.
4. What does the nervous system in humans consist of?
5. Where is brain located in man?
6. Name the important regions of human brain.
7. What are meninges?
8. Name the important parts of neuron.
9. What is autonomous nervous system?
10. Give two examples of reflex action and explain them.
11. 'Pancreas are the overall controller of the blood glucose level.' Explain.
12. Why is pituitary called the master endocrine gland?
13. Why does the freely hanging leg jerks when hit below the knee?
14. How can you justify that the pancreas and gonads perform dual role?
15. Why is nerve impulse unidirectional?
16. What are the functions of forebrain and hindbrain?
17. Adrenals are called 'stress managing glands' of the body. Give reasons.
18. What is the significance of reflex action?
19. Why hormones are called 'Chemical messengers'?
20. How is iodine important to our body?
21. How lack of growth hormone/malfunctioning of pituitary gland affects man?
22. List the different types of neuron.
23. How are spinal nerves different from cranial nerves?
24. Why are some patients of diabetes treated by giving injections of insulin?
25. In spite of not having special tissues, how is message transmitted in plants?

III. Short Answer Questions

(3 marks)

1. What is the stimulus in
   (a) phototropism (b) geotropism
   (c) chemotropism (d) thigmotropism
2. Distinguish between tropic and nastic movements of plants.
3. What is meant by receptors and effectors? Give examples of each.

4. Give the terms used for the receptors which perceive following stimulus:

   (a) smell (b) sound

   (c) light (d) taste

5. What is cerebrum? Discuss its functions.
6. Differentiate between cerebrum and cerebellum and their roles in control and coordination of the human body.
7. Name two hormones secreted by pituitary gland which are exclusively female. Discuss their functions.
8. Draw a diagram of human brain and label the following parts:

   (a) cerebrum (b) meninges

   (c) medulla oblongata (d) cerebellum

9. Define reflex action with suitable examples.
10. Write the effect of (a) excessive and (b) sluggish activity of pituitary gland.
11. What is the difference between involuntary action and reflex action?
12. Think of situations where receptors do not work properly. What problems are likely to arise?

IV. Long Answer Questions

(5 marks)

1. Describe the central nervous system in human beings.
2. Which structure in a neuron helps to conduct a nerve impulse
   (a) towards the cell body
   (b) away from the cell body?
   Explain the structure of a neuron with the help of a diagram.
3. Discuss the various functions of nervous system.
4. Describe the central nervous system of man.
5. 'Reflex action is an important activity for the survival of organisms.' Justify the statement giving three examples.
6. 'Cerebrum is the most developed part of human brain.' Discuss.
7. 'Nervous and hormonal system together perform the function of control and coordination in human beings.' Justify with the help of examples.
8. What are endocrine glands? Draw an outline of human body showing location of any five endocrine glands.
9. Discuss briefly the types of phytohormones in plants.
10. What is the need for a system of control and coordination in an organism?
11. What is the difference between the manner in which movement takes place in a sensitive plant and the movement in our legs?
12. What are the three different types of neurons? Explain their function in the nervous system of man.
13. Draw well labelled diagram of human brain.
14. Discuss the term 'tropism', explaining different types shown by plants.
15. List at least five differences between the functioning of nervous system and endocrine system.

TEST YOURSELF

Fill in the blanks

1. Receptors are structures which receive ______.
2. Endocrine glands pour their secretions in the ______.
3. The brain is enclosed in a bony box called ______.

4. The membranes covering the brain are called as ______.
5. In plants ______ movements are nondirectional while ______ movements occur in the direction of the stimulus or away from it.
6. ______ neurons carry impulse towards central nervous system while ______ neurons carry impulses away from the central nervous system.
7. Junction between two neurons is called ______.
8. ______ is an endocrine as well as an exocrine gland.
9. ______ hormone regulates metabolism of carbohydrates, fats and proteins.
10. Spontaneous, automatic and mechanical response to a stimulus is called ______.
11. Spinal cord lies in the ______ column.
12. Peripheral nervous system comprises ______ and ______ nerves.

Multiple-Choice Questions

Choose the correct option.

1. Which one of the following is geotropism?
   (a) bending of plant towards light
   (b) downward movement of root
   (c) drooping of leaves of touch-me-not plant
   (d) movement of the pollen tube

2. Phototropism refers to
   (a) bending of plant towards light
   (b) flowering of plants in response to light
   (c) a coloured pigment phytochrome
   (d) a hormone that regulates growth

3. The root of a plant is said to be
   (a) positively geotropic
   (b) positively phototropic
   (c) negatively geotropic
   (d) positively thigmotropic

4. Olfactoreceptors respond to
   (a) sound (b) touch
   (c) smell (d) taste

5. Which is not a part of the hindbrain?
   (a) cerebellum (b) pons
   (c) olfactory lobes (d) medulla oblongata

6. Which part of the human brain is highly developed?
   (a) medulla (b) cerebellum
   (c) cerebrum (d) optic lobes

7. Part of brain associated with thinking, reasoning and intelligence is
   (a) cerebellum (b) cerebrum
   (c) pons (d) medulla oblongata

8. Coordination of voluntary muscle activity is connected with
   (a) cerebrum (b) cerebellum
   (c) medulla (d) hypothalamus

9. The sequence in a simple reflex arc is as follows:
   (a) sensory neuron → receptor → motor neuron → effector
   (b) sensory neuron → receptor → spinal cord → motor neuron
   (c) receptor → sensory neuron → spinal cord → motor neuron → effector
   (d) muscle → sensory neuron → spinal cord → motor neuron

10. Which among the following is known as the master endocrine gland?
    (a) thyroid (b) pituitary
    (c) parathyroid (d) pancreas

11. Testosterone is produced by
    (a) thyroid (b) pancreas
    (c) gonads (d) pituitary

12. Which of the following is not a phytohormone?
    (a) auxins (b) propylene
    (c) ABA (d) gibberellin

13. Good smell of food causes salivation. In this example the stimulus, receptor and response respectively are
    (a) food, olfactoreceptor, salivation
    (b) smell, phonoreceptor, digestion
    (c) smell, olfactoreceptor, salivation
    (d) food, olfactoreceptor, digestion

14. Which of the following is a plant hormone?
    (a) insulin (b) thyroxin
    (c) oestrogen (d) cytokinin

15. The brain is responsible for
    (a) thinking
    (b) regulating heart beat
    (c) balancing the body
    (d) all of the above

16. Message in plants is transmitted in the form of
    (a) electrical impulse
    (b) chemical impulse
    (c) change in shape of cell
    (d) all of the above

17. Identify the odd one out:
    (a) movement of diaphragm
    (b) movement of neck
    (c) yawning
    (d) sneezing

18. Which hormone is not secreted by pituitary gland?
    (a) insulin (b) prolactin
    (c) vasopressin (d) oxytocin

Answers to Multiple-Choice Questions

1. (b)	2. (b)	3. (a)	4. (c)
5. (c)	6. (c)	7. (b)	8. (a)
9. (c)	10. (b)	11. (c)	12. (b)
13. (c)	14. (d)	15. (d)	16. (d)
17. (d)	18. (a)		

6 REPRODUCTION

Reproduction is the ability to produce other individuals of the same kind. Continuation of life in all organisms is dependent upon reproduction. It can be of two types—asexual and sexual.

DNA copying and variation

- How is it that we resemble our parents and not neighbours? How is it that the organisms look similar? The answers to all such questions lie in the inheritance of features in the form of DNA.
  - The DNA present in the cell nucleus is the source of information for making proteins.
  - During reproduction a copy of DNA is created by certain chemical reactions taking place in the reproducing cell.

    As a result, two copies of DNA are formed which need to be separated from each other.
  - The DNA copying is accompanied by the creation of an additional cellular material.
  - Out of the two DNA, one is retained in original cell and the other is pushed into the newly formed cellular apparatus. Thus, a parent cell has produced a daughter cell.
  - The two cells are similar but not absolutely identical, i.e., variations are likely to occur.
  - The extent of similarity depends on the accuracy of copying reactions. At times the variations are so drastic that the new DNA copy is non-functional. Such a daughter cell will simply die.
  - The variation produced during reproduction is the basis for evolution.
- The community of organisms in a habitat, and the non-living part of the environment make up an ecosystem.
  - Different populations have different well-defined specific places (or niches) for themselves.
  - The organisms inhabiting a particular part of ecosystem have specific body design features that allow them to use that niche. Their offspring too have a similar body design which helps their survival in that niche. The similarity in body features is due to the consistency in DNA copying during reproduction.
  - Thus DNA copying helps in the stability of populations.
  - Variation is also useful for the survival of species. If the niche of a species changes due to natural calamities, global warming, etc., the variant individuals may survive.
  - This inbuilt tendency for variation is the basis for evolution.

Asexual reproduction

- In asexual reproduction, one single individual parent gives rise to offspring which develop into new individuals. These offsprings are genetically identical to one another and to their parent. This type of reproduction takes place in unicellular organisms and animals like sponges and hydra. Modes by which various organisms reproduce depend on body design of the organism.

Activity 1

To show the growth of yeast.

1. Prepare a solution by mixing about 10 g sugar in 100 ml of water.
2. Add a pinch of yeast granules to this solution.
3. Take some of the solution in a test tube and keep it aside for few hours in a warm place.
4. This is known as yeast culture. Take few drops of yeast culture on a slide and cover it with a coverslip.
5. Observe the slide under a microscope.

Types of asexual reproduction

- **Binary Fisson** Protozoans such as *Amoeba* and *Paramoecium* undergo fission. The parent organism divides into two daughter cells and each one then grows into an adult. Fission can also be seen in bacteria, yeast and *Euglena.*

Fact file

- Most types of bacteria reproduce by **fission:** the bacterial cell splits into two. In this way solid material, such as food contaminated with bacteria, becomes covered with **colonies** as the bacterial cells multiply.
- Another example is that of *Leishmania* (which causes kala-azar) where binary fission occurs in a definite orientation due to its whip-like structure at one end of the cell.

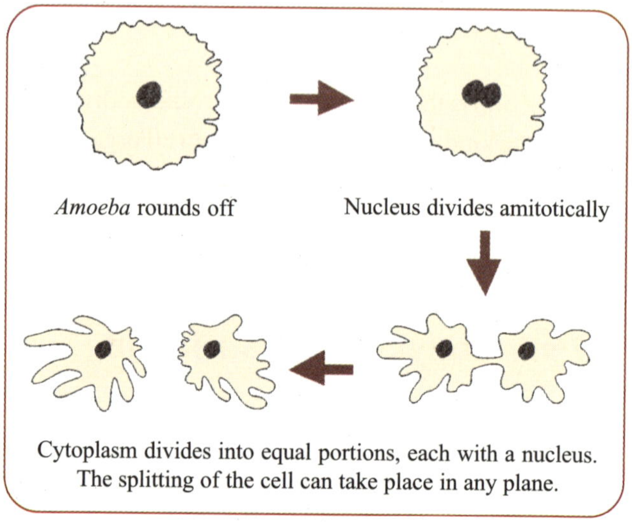

Binary fission in *Amoeba*

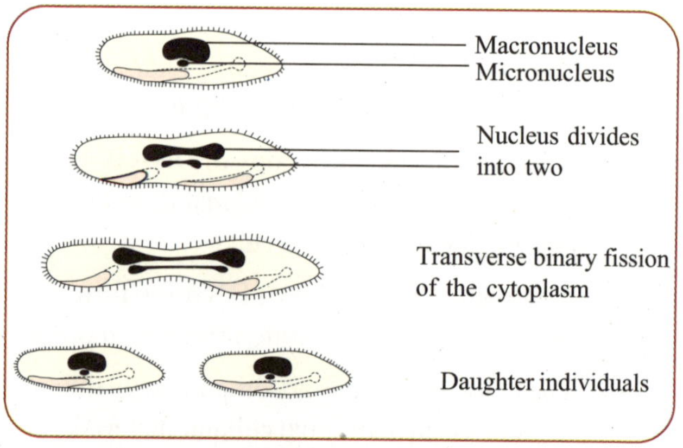

Binary fission in *Paramoecium*

- **Multiple Fission** As the name suggests, the nucleus divides repeatedly to form several daughter nuclei. Later on, each nuclei is surrounded by a small amount of cytoplasm and develops an outer membrane.Thus, many daughter cells are produced. *Plasmodium* reproduces by this method.

Differences between binary fission and multiple fission	
Binary Fission	**Multiple Fission**
• Binary fission is the simplest method of asexual reproduction. It is the division of one cell into two similar cells.	• Multiple fission occurs in unicellular organisms. It is the division of one cell into many cells.
• It occurs in favourable environmental conditions.	• It occurs in unfavourable environmental conditions.
• The nucleus divides only once amitotically into two.	• The nucleus divides repeatedly into many nuclei.
• In this division no cyst is formed.	• The organism develops a cyst under unfavourable conditions. It is the hard, protective covering over the cell.

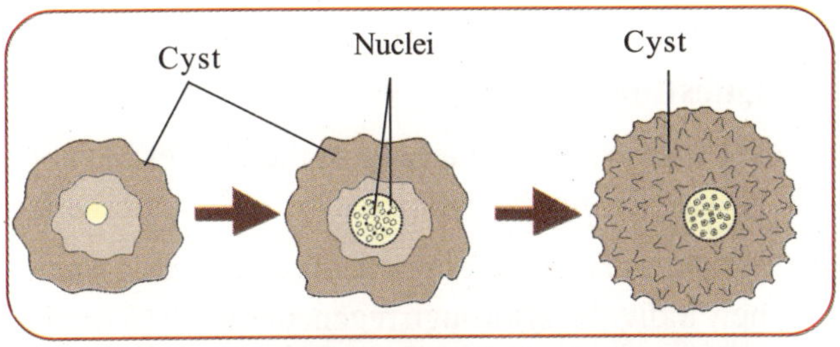

Cyst formation and multiple fission in *Plasmodium* (malarial parasite)

◆ **Budding** It may occur in both unicellular or multicellular organisms. The parent individual gives rise to a budlike projection within the body wall or cell membrane. The bud is formed as a result of repeated mitotic divisions in the parent body. It finally separates from the parent body and grows into a new individual. Budding is common in *Hydra* and sponges. In plants, yeast multiplies by repeated budding and separation.

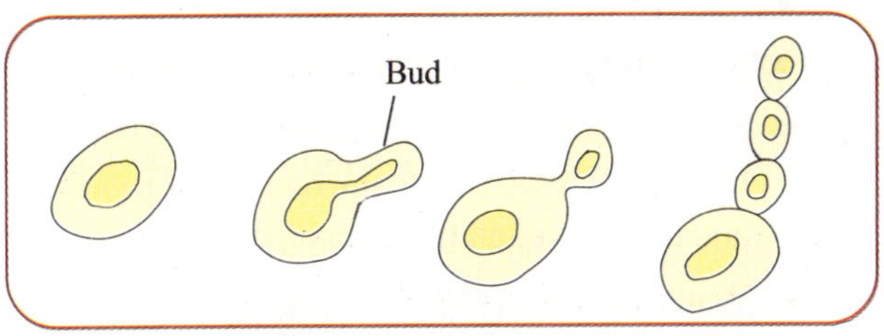

Budding in unicellular plant: *Yeast*

In yeast, a small protuberance appears on the adult cell. This grows and forms newly budded cell. Another bud appears on the tip of the newly budded cell, resulting in a chain of yeast cells.

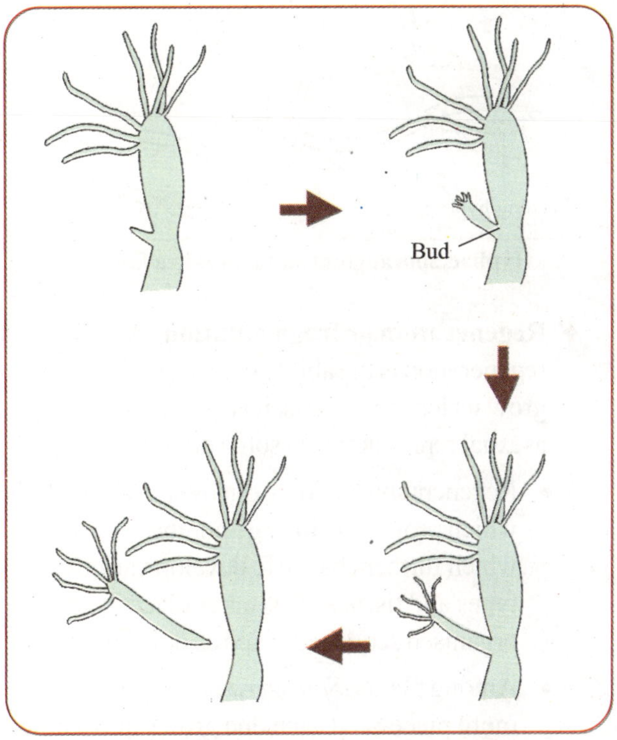

Budding in multicellular animal: *Hydra*

◆ **Spore formation** The method is commonly seen in majority of fungi and bacteria. Spore formation in the lower forms of life is one method to survive unfavourable conditions. During spore formation, a structure called **sporangium** develops from the fungal hyphae (feeding hyphae). The nucleus divides many times within the sporangium and each nucleus with bit of cytoplasm develops into a spore. Once the favourable conditions return, sporangia wall breaks and spores are released. After reaching the moist substratum spores grow into new hypha which further branches and grows to form a new individual. The common examples are *Mucor, Rhizopus* and *Penicillium.*

- Feeding hyphae are parts of the plant body that derive nutrition from the substratum. (Fungi are non-green plants).

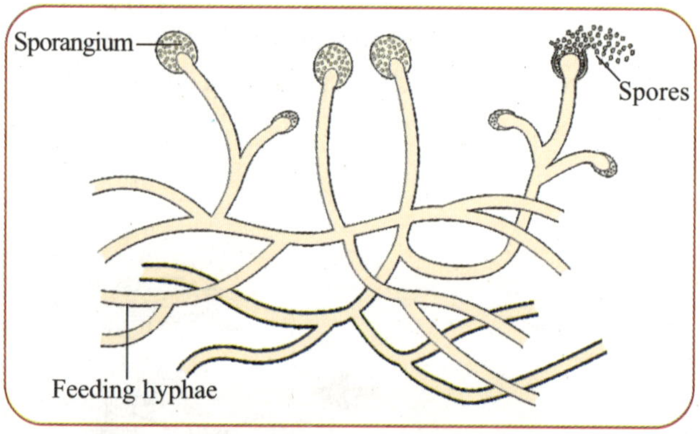

Hyphae, sporangium and spores in a fungus

◆ **Regeneration or fragmentation** Although regeneration is the ability of an organism to grow its lost body parts, it is also a method of asexual reproduction in some organisms.

- Regeneration is carried out by specialised cells which proliferate to large number of cells which further change to develop various cell types and tissues. This takes place in an organised sequence called as development.
- Among plants, *Spirogyra* breaks into two or more pieces and each one grows into a new individual. Animals like *Hydra,* flatworms *(Planaria)* and tapeworms also reproduce by this method.

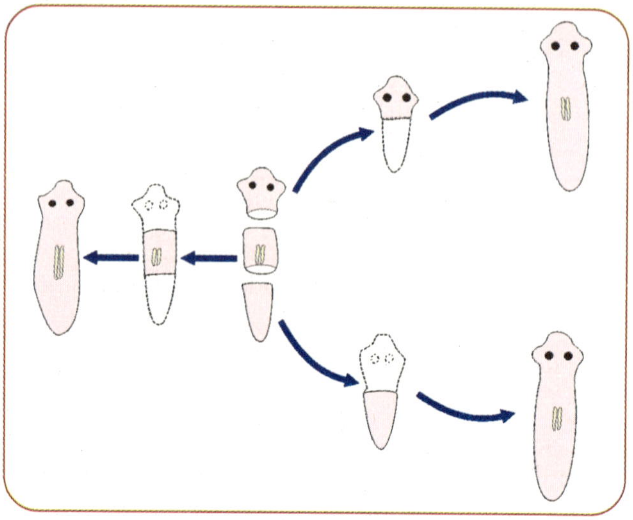

Regeneration in *Planaria*

Questions

1. Why is variation beneficial to the species but not necessarily for the individual? (2 marks)
2. Why more complex organisms cannot give rise to new individuals through regeneration? (3 marks)

Vegetative propagation

The different vegetative parts of flowering plants such as root, leaf, stem can reproduce asexually. This asexual reproduction in flowering plants is called vegetative reproduction. It is the simplest and natural method of reproduction occuring in plants.

◆ Subaerial stems like **runners** grow along the surface of the soil and produce roots where it touches the ground to give rise to a new plant.

- Strawberries produce almost leafless lateral branches called stolons, which grow roots and help in vegetative propagation.
- Water hyacinth *(Eichhornia)* propagates by subaerial lateral branch called **offset**.

The runner stem

- A stem **tuber** such as potato may sprout new shoots from its axillary buds, forming several new plants.
- The terminal bud in the **bulb** of onion gives rise to the aerial shoots.

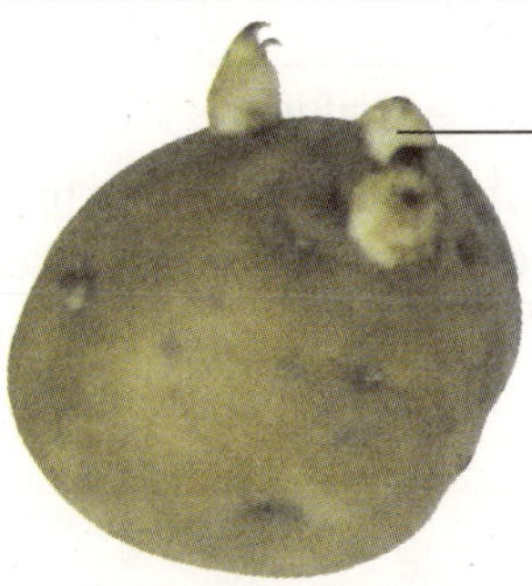

Tuber of potato

Bulb of onion

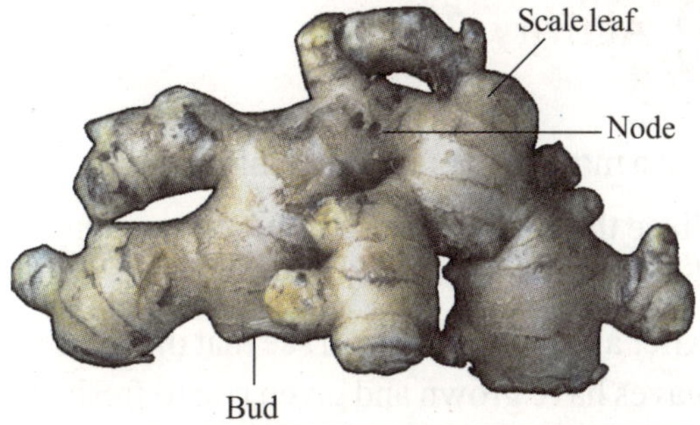

Rhizome of ginger

- **Rhizomes** such as ginger, banana and *Canna* are horizontal stems that grow from buds at the tips of the rhizomes and branch by growth of axillary buds.
- **Corms** are the condensed forms of rhizome.

Activity 2

1. Take a potato with buds on it. Cut it into small pieces so that some pieces contain a bud and some do not.
2. Place these potato pieces on a moistened cotton in a tray or plate. Observe the changes over the next few days.
3. You will see the growth of tiny plants from the pieces that contained bud.

- In plants such as *Bryophyllum,* the leaf supports development of tiny shoot buds. When the leaves fall on the ground the buds begin to form roots at their base.

Vegetative propagation by leaf (diagrammatic)

Activity 3

1. Cut a money plant into several parts.
2. Place the cut parts separately with one end dipped in water.
3. After a few days you will see that the parts having leaves have grown and given rise to fresh leaves.
   - Plants like *Dahlia* and sweet potato propagate by adventitious buds present on adventitious roots which become swollen due to storage of food.

Artificial modes of vegetative propagation

Cutting In this process, a piece of stem with some nodes and internodes is cut from a mature plant. **Adventitious** roots grow from the cut surface. Some plants like *Dahlia* are propagated by root cuttings. A cutting can also be of leaf, even a bulb scale.

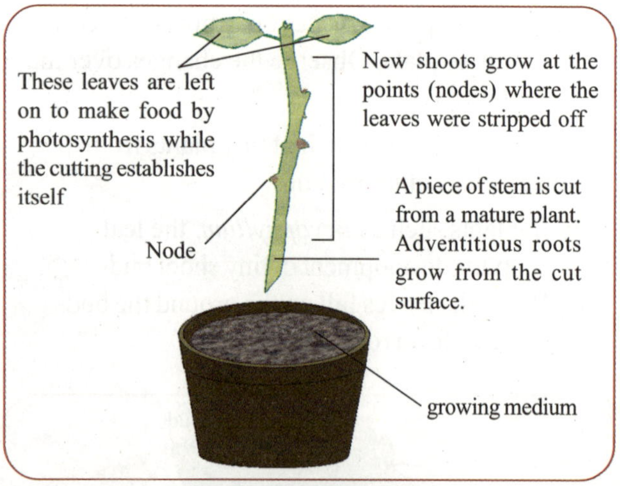

Cutting

Grafting In this method, the cutting of a plant to be reproduced **(scion)** is attached to the stem of another rooted plant **(stock)**. The cut surfaces of scion and stock are bound together in such a way that the cambia of scion and stock come in contact with each other. The joined part of the stem is then covered with wax to protect them against infection. Once the vascular systems of stock and scion are united, the scion grows on the stock. A very young scion can be made to flower when grafted on a mature stock (of a tree). Different varieties of scion can be grafted on the same stock to obtain new varieties. For example, on citrus root stock, sweet orange, lemon, lime and grape fruit can be grafted.

Grafting

Layering In this method one or more branches of the plant are bent close to the ground and covered with moist soil. The layered branches soon produce new roots and develop into separate plant while still

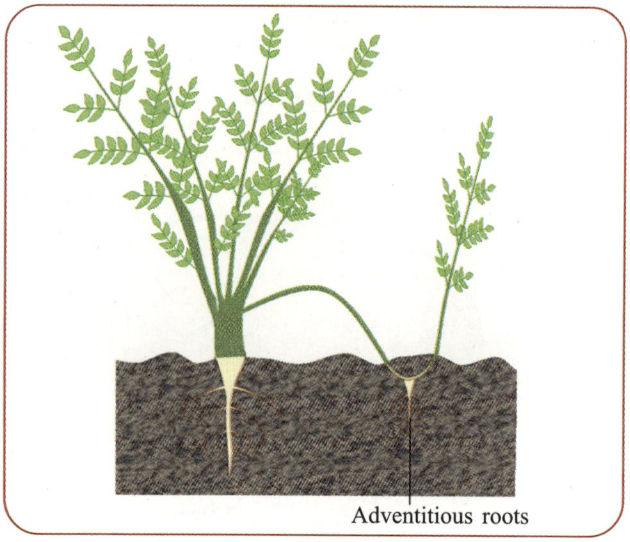

Layering

attached to the parent plant. The new plant is then separated from the parent plant and grown.

Plants in which branches cannot be bent to the ground, air layering is done. A notch of about 3 cm is made by removing bark of the stem. The scraped part is covered by moist soil and wrapped with polythene cover and tied at both ends to preserve moisture. After a few weeks rooting takes place in the scraped area. This portion is now separated from the parent plant and planted.

Air layering

Question

1. How can we obtain new varieties of citrus fruits through grafting? (2 marks)

Advantages of vegetative propagation

- Plants which do not produce seeds are propagated by this method. For example, banana, pineapple, grape, orange, jasmine and rose.
- Vegetative propagation of plants is a more rapid method than growing plants from their seeds.
- The characters of the parent plant are preserved by this method.

Different methods of vegetative propagation are used commercially for different plants.

Methods	Used for plants
• Cutting	grape, *phalsa,* rose, sugarcane, *Bougainvillea*
• Layering	raspberry, strawberry, jasmine, *Magnolia, Hibiscus,* guava, mogra, (mainly ornamental plants)
• Grafting	orange, lemon, lime, mango (mainly horticultural plants)

Parthenogenesis It is a form of reproduction in which the egg develops into a new individual without fertilisation. It is common in social insects, such as ants and honeybees where the unfertilized eggs develop into male drone.

Micropropagation It is the method used to grow plants by using a technique called **tissue culture**.

- Small fragments of plant tissue are grown in a synthetic medium that contains all the nutrients and hormones, which are needed to grow.
- Conditions are sterile.

  As a result, the new plants are free of infection.
- The tissue often develops into a fast growing cellular mass called **callus**.
- Callus is transferred to another medium for growth and differentiation and to form plantlets.
- Plantlets when transplanted into soil grow into new plants.
- The temperature is carefully controlled.

All the plants grown from pieces of one parent plant will be genetically identical. They are clones. The advantages are that the plants are healthy and retain the desirable characteristics of the parent plant. Micropropagation is a popular way of producing ornamental plants like orchids, dahlia and carnation.

Sexual reproduction

- In sexual reproduction, two individuals of different sex (male and female) give rise to a new individual.
- Though the sexual mode of reproduction involves the combining of DNA from two different indivduals, the amount of DNA in both offspring and the parents remains the same.
  - If each new generation is to be the combination of the DNA from two pre-existing individuals, then each new generation will end up having twice the amount of DNA.
- Multicellular organisms broadly have two types of cells—non-reproductive and reproductive or germ cells.
- The **germ cells** are produced in gonads by meiotic cell division. This cell division leads to the reduction of the chromosome number or the amount of DNA to half.
- During sexual reproduction, when the germ cells from two different individuals combine, the DNA content is restored thus remaining consistent in all generations.
- In simple organisms the two germ cells are quite similar.
- In complex organisms the germ cells specialise. One is fixed, large containing food reserves (female gamete). The other one is small and motile (male gamete).
- The male gametes are **sperms**. The female gametes are **ova** (*singular* ovum).
- The two different types of gametes are produced in different reproductive organs so that it leads to differences in the bodies of male and female organisms.
- Gonads are the primary sex organs in multicellular organisms. They are testes in males, and ovaries in females.
- Testes produce sperms in males and ovaries produce ova in females.
- The sperm and ova fuse—this process is called **fertilisation**. The fertilised egg cell is called a **zygote**. The zygote divides repeatedly producing a ball of cells called an **embryo** which develops into a new individual. The offspring formed by sexual reproduction inherits one of each pair of chromosomes from each parent, and are genetically different from one another and from their parents. In other words, they show **variation**.
- The DNA copying mechanisms lack in absolute accuracy and therefore give rise to variation.
- Organisms in which male and female sex organs are in different individuals are called **unisexual**. For example, higher animals and human beings.
- Organisms in which a single individual has both male and female sex organs are called **bisexual** or **hermaphrodite**.
- In plants, flower may be unisexual (papaya, watermelon) or bisexual (*Hibiscus* and mustard).
- Fertilisation can be **external** or **internal**.
- The process involving transfer of sperm from the testes into the body of female for fertilisation (fusion of sperm with the ova) to take place is called **copulation**.
- The accessory sex organs associated with copulation are copulatory organs.

The numbers on the concept map on page 82 refer to the checklist of points below.

Checklist for sexual reproduction in plants

1 ◆ Flower is the reproductive part of an angiospermic plant. The various parts of a flower are sepals, petals, stamens and carpels.

◆ **Sepals** are usually green in colour. They form the outermost whorl and protect the flower when it is in the bud.

◆ **Petals** form the inner whorl or ring next to sepals. They may be white or brightly coloured. They attract insects towards the flower and thus help in pollination.

2 ◆ **Male reproductive parts**

- **Stamens** constitute the third inner whorl. They are the male reproductive organs of the flower.
- **Anther** is the flattened top of the stamen. It produces pollen grains which are usually present as a yellow powdery substance. Reduction division takes place in pollen grains to produce male gametes. Usually, one pollen grain produces two male gametes.
- **Filament** is the stalk with an anther on its tip.

◆ **Female reproductive parts**

- **Pistil** is the centrally placed fourth whorl. It bears the female reproductive organ called carpel.
- **Carpel** consists of an ovary bearing a style and a stigma.
- **Stigma** is a flattened disclike structure at the top of the style. Its tip is sticky so that pollen grains stick to it.
- **Style** is an elongated tubelike structure. It connects the stigma to the ovary.
- **Ovary** contains ovules and each ovule has an egg cell in it which is the female gamete.

◆ In flowering plants, sexual reproduction involves **pollination, fertilisation** and the formation of **fruits** and **seeds**.

◆ **Pollination** is the transfer of pollen from the anther to the stigma. Mature pollen grains are shed from the anther and reach the stigma of either the same, or another flower.

◆ **Cross-pollination** is the transfer of pollen from anthers to stigma(s) of different plant(s).

◆ **Self-pollination** is the transfer of pollen from the anthers to stigma(s) on the same plant. Many agents like wind, water and insects help to transfer pollen grains.

3 ◆ **Fertilisation in a flowering plant**

It is the fusion of a male sex nucleus with the female egg nucleus.

◆ From the pollen grain on reaching stigma, forms the pollen tube from one of the pores of the pollen grain wall. Two male gametes are also formed.

◆ The pollen tube grows down the style and enters a small hole, the **micropyle** in an ovule.

◆ The two male gametes from the pollen tube are released into the embryo sac.

◆ Fertilisation occurs in the embryo sac where nucleus of a male gamete (n) fuses with the egg nucleus (n) to form a zygote (2n)—**syngamy**.

◆ At the same time, the second male nucleus (n) enters the embryo sac and fuses with the endosperm nucleus (2n) or two polar nuclei—**triple fusion**.

The mechanism of two fusions i.e., syngamy and triple fusion occuring in an embryo sac is called **double fertilisation**.

Triple fusion leads to the formation of endosperm which ensures food reserve for the embryo plant in the seed.

SEXUAL REPRODUCTION IN PLANTS

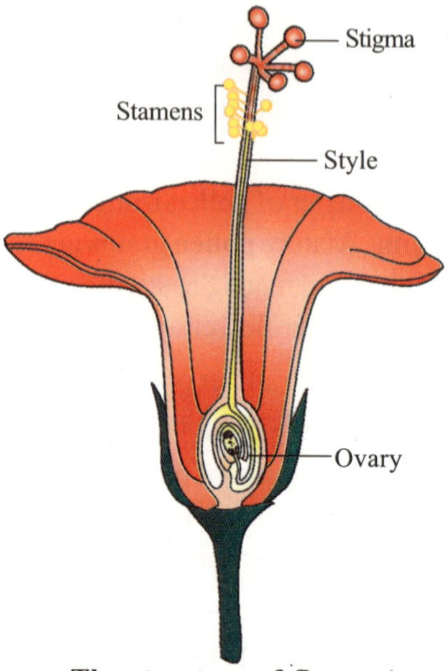

The structure of flower (two sepals and two petals removed)

A sepal

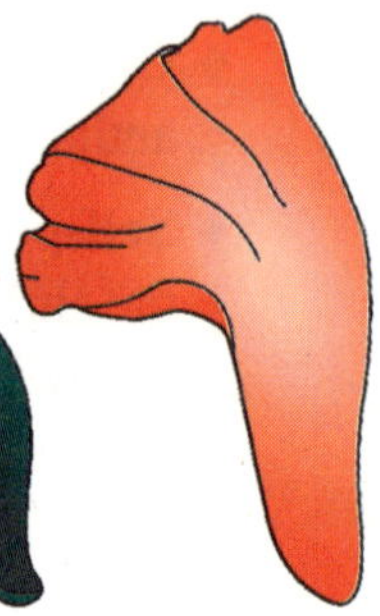

A petal

The flower—reproductive part of a plant

CHECK LIST 1

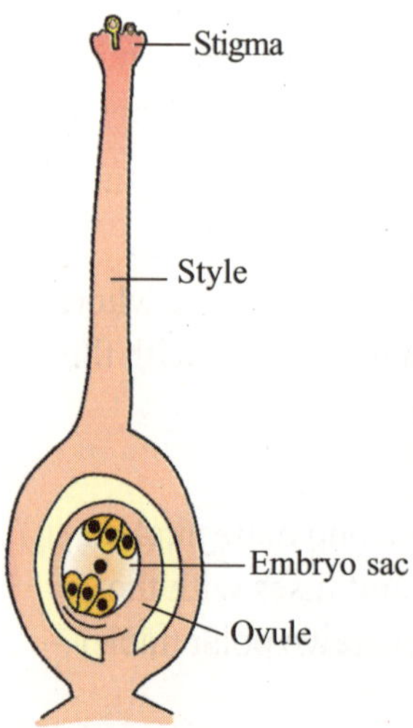

The carpel

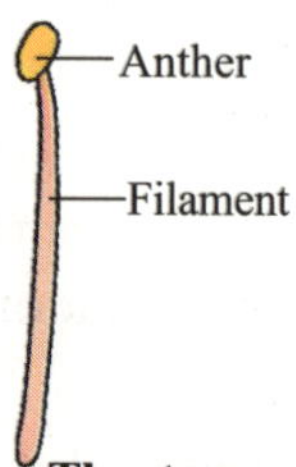

The stamen

CHECK LIST 2

CHECK LIST 3

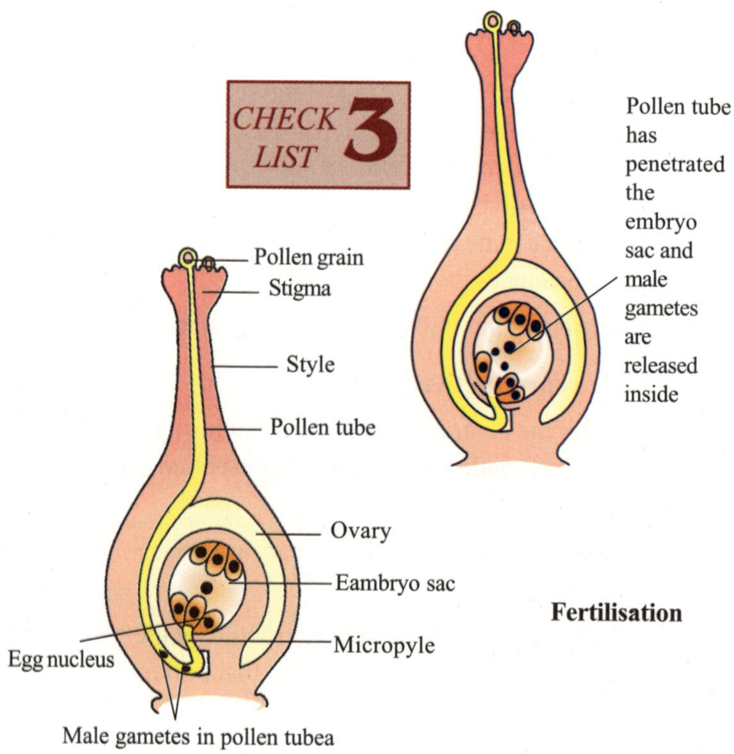

Fertilisation

After fertilisation, ovary develops into fruits and ovules develop into seeds. Petals, sepals, style and stigma may fall off.

- The seed contains the baby plant or embryo which develops into a seedling under appropriate conditions. This process is known as **germination**.

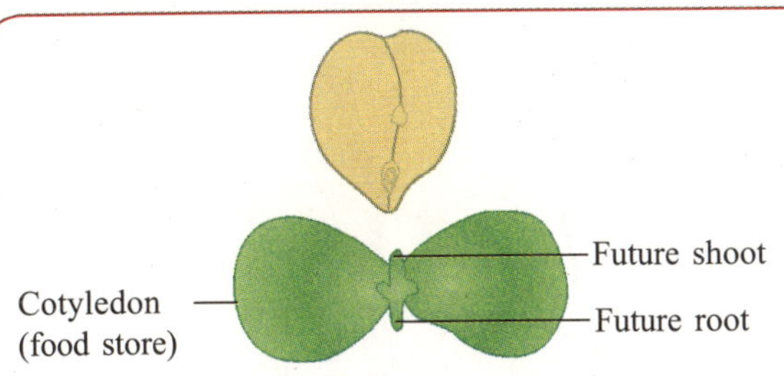

Germination

Human reproductive system

Reproductive system is highly evolved in humans (mammals). Humans are unisexual with separate male and female individuals. The primary sexual organs (gonads) produce sperms and ova.

- The reproductive system in the life of human beings becomes functional at a definite age called **puberty**.
  - Males attain puberty at the age of 13 to 14 years while females attain it at the age of 10 to 12 years.
  - Besides producing gametes the gonads are also endocrine glands producing sex hormones.

The hormones perform several functions. They

- regulate the process of gametogenesis, i.e., formation of sperm and ovum.
- maintain the structure and function of accessory sex organs.
- develop secondary sex characters like pitch of the voice, growth of facial, axial and pubic hair, and development of mammary glands. Skin beomes oily and develop pimples.

The numbers on the concept map on pages 84–85 refer to the checklist of points below.

Checklist for human reproductive system

1 ◆ **Male Reproductive System** It includes following organs:

- **Testis** is the primary, male reproductive organ. There are two testes each contained in the scrotum. The testes produce sperms continuously from the stage of puberty. It also produces male hormone testosterone which brings about changes in appearance in a boy.
- **Scrotum** is the small sac like muscular structure outside the abdominal cavity. It provides an optimal temperature (which is 1–3° lower than the temperature of the body) for the formation of sperms.
- **Vas deferens** is a long tube arising from each of the **testes**. It runs anteriorly up to the urinary bladder and connects with urethra just below the bladder.
- Prostate glands and seminal vesicles are present along the path of vas deferens. They both add their secretions to vas deferens carrying sperms. Thus, sperms move in fluid state which makes their passage easy. This fluid also provides nutrition.
  - Sperms are tiny bodies consisting mainly of genetic material and a tail which helps them to move towards female germ cell.
- **Urethra** is enclosed within a thick muscular organ, penis. It opens to the outside through a male genital pore which is one common opening

THE HUMAN REPRODUCTIVE SYSTEM

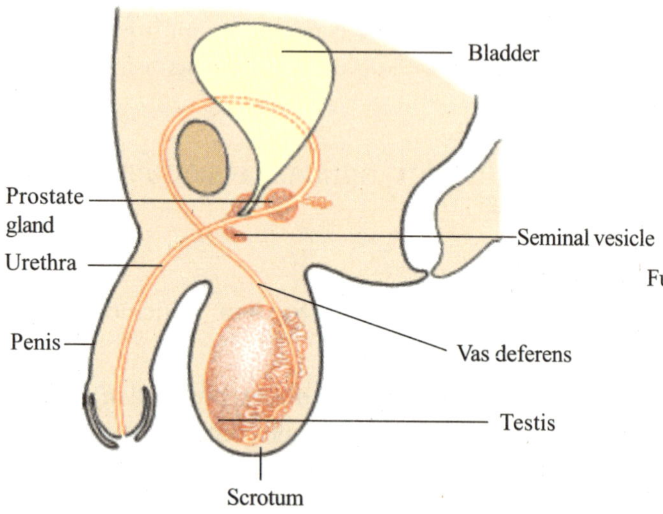

The male reproductive organs

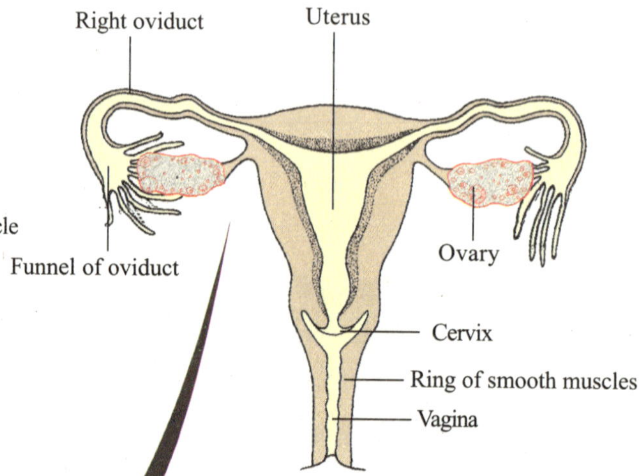

The female reproductive organs

CHECK LIST 1

CHECK LIST 2

CHECK LIST 3

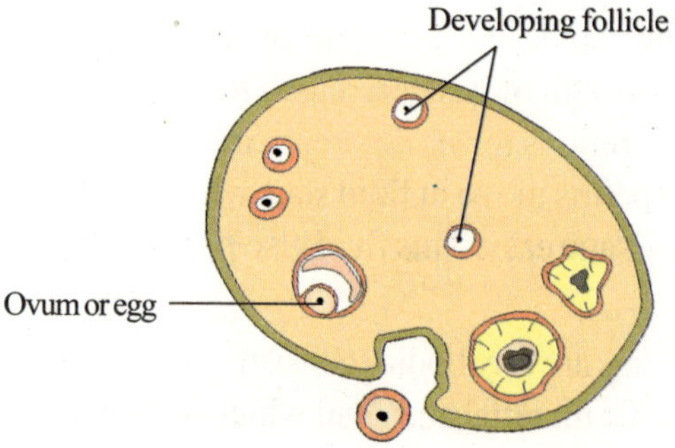

Ovulation—egg is released from its follicle

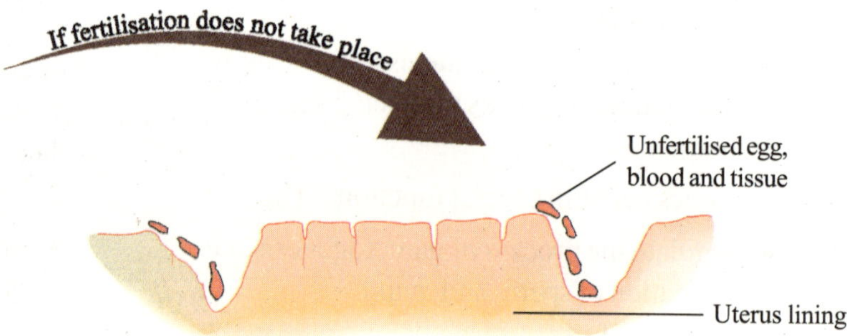

Lining of uterus breaks down if fertilisation does not take place; blood and tissue pass through vagina as menstrual flow

If fertilisation takes place after ovulation

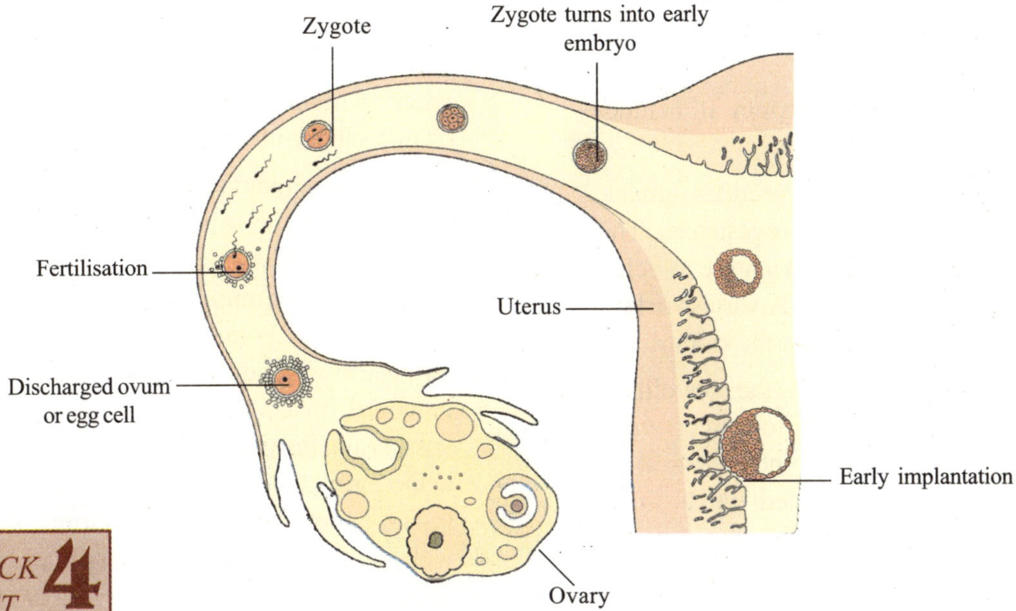

CHECK LIST 4

Fertilisation and implantation

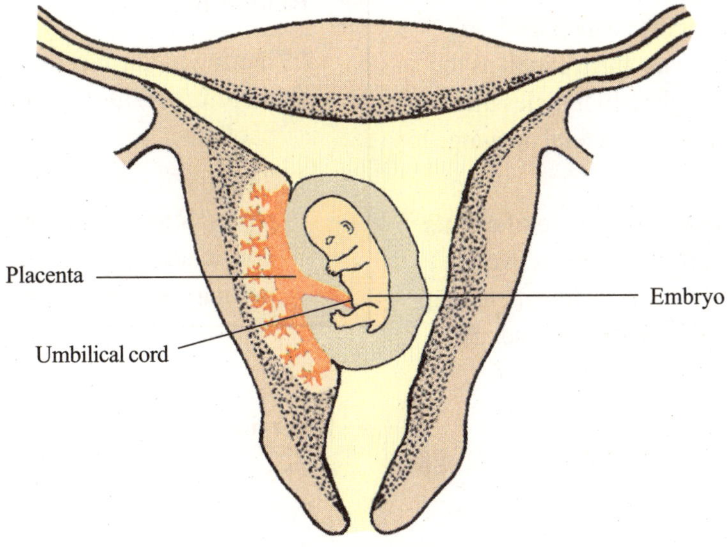

CHECK LIST 5

Human embryo in the uterus

for the urine and sperms. Therefore male reproductive system is called **urinogenital system**.

- **Penis** is the muscular and tubular organ used during copulation.

2 ◆ **Female Reproductive System** It includes following organs:

- **Ovary** produces eggs and secretes female hormones—estrogen and progesterone. The eggs or ova are produced in mature follicles inside the ovary. The paired ovaries are located in the abdominal cavity near the kidney.
- **Oviduct (fallopian tube)** is the convoluted tube located near the posterior end of ovary, down which the ova pass when released from the ovary. It has the expanded, funnel-shaped opening close to each ovary.
- **Uterus** is a pear-shaped muscular structure. The two oviducts from each ovary open into the upper broader portion of the uterus. The fertilized ovum develops into a baby inside the uterus.
- **Cervix** is the lower narrow portion of the uterus which consists of the ring of muscles.
- **Vagina** is a tubular structure which leads to outside. It is also known as 'birth canal' as the young one is born through it. In females the urinary opening (urethra) and genital opening (vagina) are separate.

3 ◆ **Sexual cycle in females** The cycle of events taking place in the ovaries and uterus every twenty eight days and marked by the menstrual or sexual flow is called **menstrual** or sexual cycle. (There is no such cycle in case of males.)

- The ovaries contain thousands of immature eggs from birth. On reaching puberty eggs start maturing.
- In a human female the ovarian follicles grow into mature follicle which develops to surround one ovum or egg. A single egg normally produced is discharged **(ovulation)** from one of the two ovaries each month from **menarche** until the **menopause**.
- **Menarche** is the first menstruation at puberty whereas **menopause** is the stoppage of cyclic changes in the uterus and no menstruation.
- Maturation of ovarian follicle and thickening of uterus wall occur simultaneously. The inner wall of uterus (by thickening) prepares itself to receive the developing zygote and provide nourishment to embryo if fertilisation occurs. If fertilisation does not take place, the thickened inner wall breaks down alongwith its blood vessels and flow out of the body through vagina in the form of bleeding called menstrual flow. It lasts for about 4–7 days. In a normal healthy woman, ovulation takes place around 14th day of the cycle.
- The period between menarche and menopause is the normal reproductive life in human female. (12 to 50 years).

> ☞ **Remember**
>
> * During pregnancy there is no ovulation and therefore no menstruation till the birth of the baby.
>
> * The functions of the ovary and other reproductive organs are controlled by hormones released from hypothalamus, pituitary and female hormones.

4 ◆ **Fertilisation and implantation**

- The semen from the penis is ejaculated into the vagina during sexual intercourse. The process is also known as mating or copulation.
- There are millions of sperms in the semen which are highly mobile and active, they pass through

the uterus and enter the oviduct. The sperms are tiny bodies with a long tail which helps in their motility.

- If there is an ovum in the oviduct, one of the sperm enters the ovum and the male nucleus fuses with the female nucleus. This is called **fertilisation**.
- The fertilized ovum or zygote is formed only when the copulation takes place during ovulatory period.
- The zygote once formed undergoes repeated mitotic cell divisions to form an early embryo as it moves down the fallopian tube.
- The early embryo travels down the fallopian tube to the uterus.
- Implantation occurs when the early embryo sinks into the lining of the uterus.

5 - Soon after implantation, an organ called **placenta** develops between uterine wall and the embryo (foetus). The **umbilical cord**, arising from the embryo's abdomen, serves as a link between the embryo and the placenta. The placenta is the site of exchange of nutrients and waste products between maternal and embryo blood circulations.

- The foetus develops inside the uterus till birth. The total period of embryonic development from the time of fertilisation to birth is called gestation. It is around 280 days in humans. It is calculated from the first day of the last menstrual cycle.
- **Parturition** is the birth of the fully developed foetus on completion of gestation. The child is born as a result of rhythmic contractions of uterine muscles. The newly born normal child weighs about 3.5 kg.

Remember

* The functions of the ovary and other reproductive organs are controlled by hormones released from hypothalamus and pituitary.

Questions

1. Explain the term hermaphrodite with the help of an example. (2 marks)
2. What happens to an egg cell if fertilisation does not take place? (2 marks)

Population control by contraception

- **Contraception** aims to prevent pregnancy by preventing
  - sperm from reaching the egg, or
  - eggs from being produced, or
  - the fertilised egg from developing in the uterus.

Three methods used for contraception are broadly categorised as:

- **Barrier** They prevent the sperm from reaching the egg during copulation. Condom, diaphragm and cervical caps are the physical devices used for this purpose.
- **Chemical method** It prevents eggs from being produced. Oral pills used for this purpose are mainly hormonal preparations and are called **oral contraceptives** (OCs). They stop the production of gametes (ova) by the action on hypothalamus, pituitary and the ovaries.

- **Surgical methods** They include the use of **Intrauterine Contraceptive Devices (IUCDs)**. A copper-T is placed safely inside the uterus, which prevents implantation in the uterus. Some other surgical methods include removal or ligation of a small portion of vas deferens in male **(vasectomy)** and the fallopian tube in female **(tubectomy)**. The use of contraceptives has side effects. Therefore, awareness and regular medical advise is necessary.

Reproductive health and sexually transmitted diseases

Health is a state of complete physical, mental and social wellbeing. Reproductive health includes certain aspects like a responsible, safe and satisfying reproductive life. It also includes

- awareness among males and females regarding the fertility regulation methods
- the right, the freedom and choice to control child birth
- the ability to prevent and control sexually transmitted diseases
- to manage disorders related to the reproductive system.

The sexually transmitted diseases are a group of communicable diseases that are transmitted predominantly by sexual contact. They are caused by a variety of bacterial, viral, protozoal or fungal agents.

- Common STDs are gonorrhea, syphilis and trichomoniases. The symptoms are burning sensation at urination and urethral discharge. These diseases are curable.
- Viral infections like warts and AIDS are also STDs causing death. The causative agent for this disease is Human Immunodeficiency Virus (HIV).

World Health Organisation (WHO) has now considered reproductive health as a fundamental human right. The National Population Policy and National Health Policy covers these aspects under their programmes. NGOs too share the responsibility of bringing awareness.

Differences between pollination and fertilisation

Pollination	Fertilisation
• The transfer of pollen from the anther to the stigma is called pollination.	• Fertilisation is the fusion of male and female gametes.
• The process involves many external agencies such as wind and air.	• The process occurs inside the organism's body and does not involve any external agency.
• Pollination followed by fertilisation leads to the development of a new individual.	• Fertilisation alone can lead to the development of a new individual.

EXERCISES

I. Very Short Answer Questions

(1 mark)

1. Define reproduction.
2. What is essential for an organism to reproduce by sexual method?
3. Name any two organisms that show asexual reproduction.
4. What is a spore?
5. Name any two plants that reproduce through spores.
6. What is binary fission?
7. How is multiple fission different from binary fission?
8. Define regeneration.
9. Name two organisms which reproduce by regeneration.
10. Name the type of reproduction that does not involve gametes.
11. Define callus.
12. Name any two plants produced by tissue culture method.
13. How is grafting useful in plants?
14. What are scion and stock?
15. Suggest one limitation of vegetative propagation.
16. What is parthenogenesis?
17. What is meant by bisexual organism?
18. If a plant does not produce seeds, how can it be propagated?
19. In terms of sex organs, what is common between a tapeworm and an earthworm?
20. Suggest one advantage of sexual reproduction.
21. Name the reproductive parts of a flower.
22. What is the function of petals in a flower?
23. What is the yellow powdery substance present in the anther of a flower?
24. Define pollination.
25. What is fertilisation?
26. What is the fate of ovule and ovary after fertilisation?
27. Name the biotic agencies of pollination.
28. What is syngamy?
29. What is formed when male gamete fuses with female gamete?
30. Name the tiny opening in ovule through which male gamete enters.
31. What is the stage of development between the zygote and newly formed baby called as?
32. Give the other name of sex cells.
33. What is triple fusion?
34. Define the term 'Puberty'.
35. What is the age of puberty in human males and human females?
36. Why are testes in human males placed outside the body?
37. Name the male and female gonads in human beings.
38. What are the dual purposes served by urethra in man?

39. Name the tube that arises from each of the testis in a human male.
40. Where does conception occur in human females?
41. Where does a fertilised ovum develops into a baby in the human body?
42. Which comes earlier menarche or menopause?
43. Define menarche.
44. What is menopause?
45. How long does a menstrual cycle last in human females?
46. Trace the path of sperms in a human female.
47. In which situation other than menopause the ovulation and menstruation can stop in a woman?
48. Which organ enables the developing foetus to obtain nourishment from the mother's blood?
49. Which part of the human female body is called as 'birth canal'?
50. What exactly happens when a woman undergoes tubectomy?
51. Suggest one surgical method of birth control in men.
52. Expand AIDS.
53. Name some common STDs.

II. Short Answer Questions

(2 marks)

1. What are the two types of reproduction and how are they different from each other?
2. List various ways of asexual reproduction in organisms.
3. Why is reproduction essential for the survival of species?
4. How does *Hydra* reproduce?
5. Explain the process of binary fission in *Amoeba*.
6. Where are spores borne? Where do such structures exist?
7. What is the significance of pollination?
8. List the basic features of sexual reproduction which are not seen in asexual reproduction.
9. How grafting is considered a common method of obtaining a superior plant from two different plants?
10. What would have been the consequence in terms of evolution if there was no sexual reproduction in the entire living world?
11. Differentiate between self-pollination and cross-pollination.
12. Explain the term double fertilisation. What is its significance?
13. Briefly define the term unisexual and bisexual giving one example each.
14. How is internal fertilisation different from external fertilisation?
15. What are accessory sex organs?
16. Summarize the process of formation of the placenta. What is its significance?
17. Mention two changes that occur simultaneously with the follicular maturation in human females.
18. Why is that the probability of fertilisation is more if mating takes place during the middle of the sexual cycle in human females?
19. What are STDs? Give two examples.
20. State the function of fallopian tube in human female body.
21. How is male reproductive system different from female reproductive system in humans?

III. Short Answer Questions

(3 marks)

1. Which endocrine glands control the functions of the ovary and other reproductive organs? Explain.
2. Define the term layering. What are its two types?
3. Which type of pollination is likely to promote variation? Give reasons.
4. Why are sperms produced in much large number than ova?
5. Describe the technique of tissue culture.
6. What happens to ovarian cycle if pregnancy sets in?
7. Broadly classify the methods of contraception.
8. Label the given diagram. What is the diagram representing?

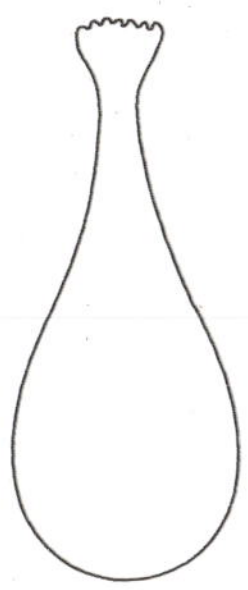

9. Give the full forms of
   (a) HIV
   (b) OC
   (c) IUCD.
10. How do barrier methods prevent fertilisation?
11. How do oral contraceptives affect the female reproductive system?
12. What are the common symptoms of sexually transmitted diseases?
13. Differentiate between vasectomy and tubectomy.
14. List the agencies that help in making people aware of reproductive health.
15. Differentiate between ureter and urethra in humans.
16. What do you mean by reproductive health? Why its awareness is important?
17. Explain the various steps of budding in *Hydra* with the help of a diagram.
18. Why is the male reproductive system called as 'urinogenital system'?
19. Explain the various steps to be followed to perform layering on jasmine plant.
20. Describe the secondary sexual characters in human male and female.
21. Describe the surgical methods of birth control.
22. Discuss the role of hormones involved in reproductive system of humans.
23. How does reproduction help in providing stability to populations of species?
24. Can an unfertilised egg form a new organism in the sexually reproducing type of organisms? Define the two terms associated with it.
25. Name the methods that a gardener would employ to propagate the following plants:
    (a) *Bryophyllum* (b) Rose
    (c) Jasmine (d) Grape.
26. Explain sexual cycle in human females. What is menstrual flow? Which term signifies cessation of the cycle?

IV. Long Answer Questions

(5 marks)

1. Discuss the various types of reproduction in organisms. Give examples for each type.
2. With the help of a labelled diagram describe the process of binary fission in *Amoeba.*
3. With the help of diagrams, discuss the process of budding in yeast.

4. Giving suitable examples, discuss the three commonest methods of artificial propagation.
5. Define grafting. How is it done? Suggest two advantages and two disadvantages of this method.
6. Explain vegetative propagation in plants. What are its advantages?
7. Draw a well labelled diagram of a flower showing its various parts.
8. What do you mean by double fertilisation? Enumerate the steps involved in fertilisation in a flowering plant. Give suitable diagrams.
9. Describe the process of tissue culture. What are its advantages.
10. Briefly discuss the male reproductive system in humans.
11. Enumerate the events of female menstrual cycle, starting from the maturation of follicles.
12. Describe the events that occur after the process of fertilisation till parturition in the human female body.
13. Draw a well labelled diagram of female reproductive system in humans describing various structures.
14. Draw male reproductive system showing following parts:
    (a) Testis (b) Urethra
    (c) Vas deferens (d) Penis.

15 How are modes for reproduction different in unicellular and multicellular organisms?

TEST YOURSELF

Fill in the blanks

1. Bulb is a type of underground ______.
2. In a seed, the embryo is diploid but the endosperm is ______.
3. In rose many types of flowers can be obtained on a single plant. It is possible due to the process of ______.
4. During asexual reproduction, the cell divisions are ______.
5. Spore formation occurs in structures called ______.
6. In grafting the portion of plant grafted on the other is called ______ while the plant in which grafting is done is called ______.
7. Gametes are produced in ______ by ______ division.
8. The cells involved in sexual reproduction are called ______.
9. An organism having both male and female reproductive organs is called ______.
10. The product of syngamy is ______.
11. Ovulation occurs around ______ day of ovarian cycle.
12. ______ from each of the ovary opens into the uterus.
13. The gestation period in human beings is ______ days.
14. IUCD prevents ______ in uterus.
15. After attaining puberty ovaries and uterus undergo cyclic changes every ______ days.

Multiple-Choice Questions

Choose the correct option.

1. The part of sugarcane used for vegetative propagation is
   (a) root (b) stem
   (c) leaf (d) flower

2. When an organism breaks into a number of parts and each part grows into a new individual, it is called
   (a) budding (b) binary fission
   (c) regeneration (d) spore formation

3. During grafting, the portion of a plant that is grafted is called
   (a) scion (b) stock
   (c) stalk (d) stem

4. Development of an organism from an unfertilised ovum is called
   (a) vegetative propagation (b) parthenogenesis
   (c) oogensis (d) asexual reproduction

5. Which of the following produces male gametes in a flower?
   (a) sepals (b) petals
   (c) stamens (d) carpels

6. During pollination, pollen gains get carried to which part of the carpel?
   (a) style (b) stigma
   (c) ovary (d) ovule

7. Which part of the flower grows to form the fruit after fertilisation?
   (a) stamens
   (b) carpels
   (c) ovule
   (d) ovary

8. The number of male gametes in the pollen tube, at the time of entering into an ovule is
   (a) two (b) four
   (c) three (d) one

9. Which of the following is a male hormone?
   (a) testosterone (b) oestrogen
   (c) progesterone (d) FSH

10. Implantation of embryo takes place in the
    (a) fallopian tubes (b) uterus
    (c) ovary (d) vagina

11. Average duration of human pregnancy is calculated from
    (a) the first day of last menstrual cycle
    (b) the last day of expected menstrual cycle
    (c) the day of ovulation
    (d) the day of conception

12. Which of the following is a hormonal preparation for birth control?
    (a) diaphragm (b) oral pills
    (c) cervical cap (d) tubectomy

13. Which of the following is not a sexually transmitted disease?
    (a) syphilis (b) gonorrhoea
    (c) AIDS (d) TB

14. Which of the following is an IUCD?
    (a) copper-T (b) oral pills
    (c) diaphragm (d) tubectomy

15. HIV causes
    (a) syphilis (b) gonorrhoea
    (c) AIDS (d) TB

Answers to Multiple-Choice Questions

1. (b)	2. (c)	3. (a)	4. (b)
5. (c)	6. (b)	7. (d)	8. (a)
9. (a)	10. (b)	11. (a)	12. (b)
13. (d)	14. (a)	15. (c)	

7 HEREDITY AND EVOLUTION

All living organisms breed their kind. Sparrow's egg hatch into a sparrow but never into crow or some other bird. This means that the characteristics of a species are passed down from one generation to another. Thus, **heredity** is the transmission of traits from parents to offspring.

- The information for heredity is present in the fertilised egg or zygote which is formed in sexual reproduction only.
- **Variation** is defined as the occurrence of differences among the individuals. Notice the different coloured hair and eyes among your classmates. We all show variations in the different characteristics. Variation arises from genetic causes.
- **Genetics** is called the science of heredity and variation, as it involves both.

Accumulation of variation during reproduction

◆ The characters are passed on from one generation to another with slight variations. The variations when get accumulated in generations become apparent as newly created diifferences. The extent of variation in an organism depends on how it has been reproduced.

- In **asexual reproduction**, the similarities among all individuals belonging to the same line of descent are preserved with slight variations due to small inaccuracies in DNA copying.
- In **sexual reproduction** both similarity and variation is observed even among offspring; therefore chances of greater diversity exist.

◆ The chances of survival of variations in different organisms is not the same.Variations can be advantageous or disadvantageous for an organism. The chance of survival of variations are influenced by the environmental factors.

- The environment of an organism means every factor which influences the organism from outside.
- The selection of variations by environmental factors forms the basis of evolution. For example, bacteria that can withstand heat will survive.

Heredity

The concept of heredity is as old as the ancient civilisation of Babylon and Assyria when selective breeding of horses and cattle was done. Ancient chinese writings mention about creating better varities of paddy. Charaka (100 BC), the ancient Indian medical practitioner knew the factors that determine the sex of a child.

After the invention of microscope in the 17th century, it was evident that gametes provide the physical basis of heredity.

Activity 1

Study variation in the earlobes (whether attached or free) of students of your class and correlate the type of earlobe of each student with that of his/her parents.

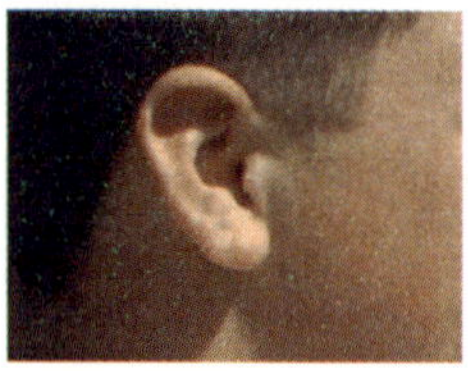

A

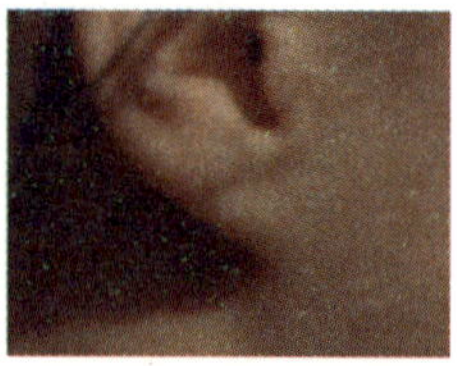

B

Procedure

1. Observe the ears of all the students in your class and prepare two separate lists of students having free or attached earlobes.
2. Find out the percentage of each type.
3. Find out the earlobe of the parents of each student and record.
4. Correlate the earlobe type of each student with that of their parents.
5. Study the record and draw a conclusion regarding a possible rule for inheritance of earlobe types.

Rules for the inheritance of traits—Mendel's contributions

- As you know, in sexual reproduction, both the father and the mother contribute practically equal amount of genetic material.

  For example, suppose the mother has blue eyes and the father brown eyes. The child might receive a gene for blue eyes from its mother and a gene for brown eyes from its father. If this happens, the child will have brown eyes, as the gene for brown eyes is said to be **dominant** to the gene for blue eyes. Although the gene for blue eyes is present in all the child's cells, it is not expressed. It is **recessive** to brown.
- The scientific principles governing the pattern of inheritance were known only after the experimental findings of Mendel.
- **Gregor Johann Mendel** (1822–1884) was a monk at the town of Brunn. He observed the inheritance of contrasting characters in the garden pea (*Pisum sativum*) and reported the results of his experiments in 1865.
- Mendel in his simple experiments, crossed pure-bred pea plants having contrasting characters like round/wrinkled seeds, tall/short plants and white/violet flowers. He found that in the first generation only one character appeared which is dominant. But in the second generation both characters appeared. This means that one character (which appeared in the second generation) must have been hidden or masked in the first generation.
- The results led Mendel to interpret that the inheritance of contrasting characters was controlled by units which he called 'factors'. The work established the basis of modern genetics. However, at that time, nobody realised what Mendel was talking about. Nothing was known about the factors of chromosome and DNA at that time. Mendel's experimental findings got recognition only in the year 1900, many years after his death. Mendel's 'factors' are what we know today as 'genes'. The term **'gene'** was coined by **Johanssen** in 1909.

Important terms related to genetics

- **Pure breeding**—characteristics that breed true, appearing unchanged generation after generation.

- **First filial generation** (symbol $\mathbf{F_1}$)—the offspring produced by the parents.
- **Second filial generation** (symbol $\mathbf{F_2}$)—the offspring produced by crossing members of the first filial generation.
- **Gene**—a length of DNA which codes for one protein, one of a pair of genes control a particular characteristic.
- **Gene expressed**—a gene is expressed when a protein is produced from the activity of the gene.
- **Dominant**—any characteristic that appears in the F_1 offspring of a cross between pure-breeding parants with contrasting characteristics, such as tallness and shortness in pea plants.
- **Recessive**—any characteristic present in the parental generation that does not appear in the F_1 generation but reappears in the F_2 generation.

Important rules related to genetics

- Letters are used to symbolise genes.
- A capital letter is used to symbolise the dominant member of a pair of genes.
- A small letter is used to symbolise the recessive member of a pair of genes.
- The letter used to symbolise the recessive gene is the same letter as that for the dominant gene.
- In the tall parent plant, every gamete carries the trait **T** which controls tallness.
- In the short (dwarf) parent plant, every gamete carries the allele **t** which controls shortness (dwarfness).
- All F_1 plants are tall, because **T** is the dominant character which masks the effect of the recessive **t**. Each F_1 plant produces two types of gametes. 50% of gametes carry the **T** trait, the other 50% carry the **t** trait.

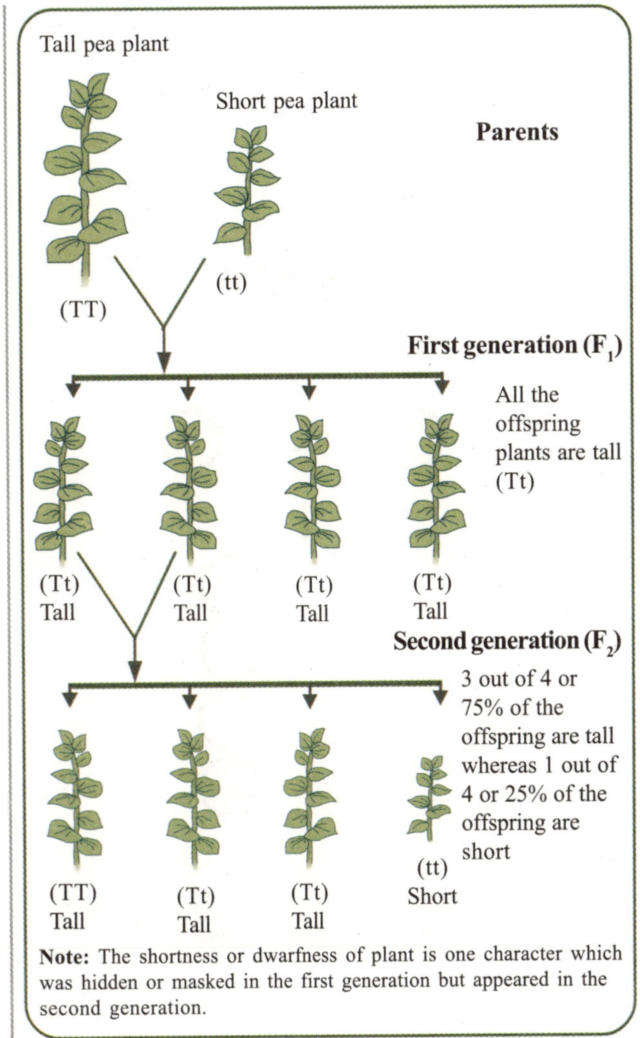

Mendel's experiment to show that inheritance of contrasting characters (here height of plant) was controlled by units called factors

- In the F_2 generation not all the tall plants have the same combination of traits. 50% of the plants have both dominant and recessive traits (Tt), 25% are pure tall **(TT)**, and the remaining 25% are short **(tt)**.
- Now let us discuss an experiment in which Mendel considered two different characteristics (say shape and colour of seeds) of pea plants at a time.

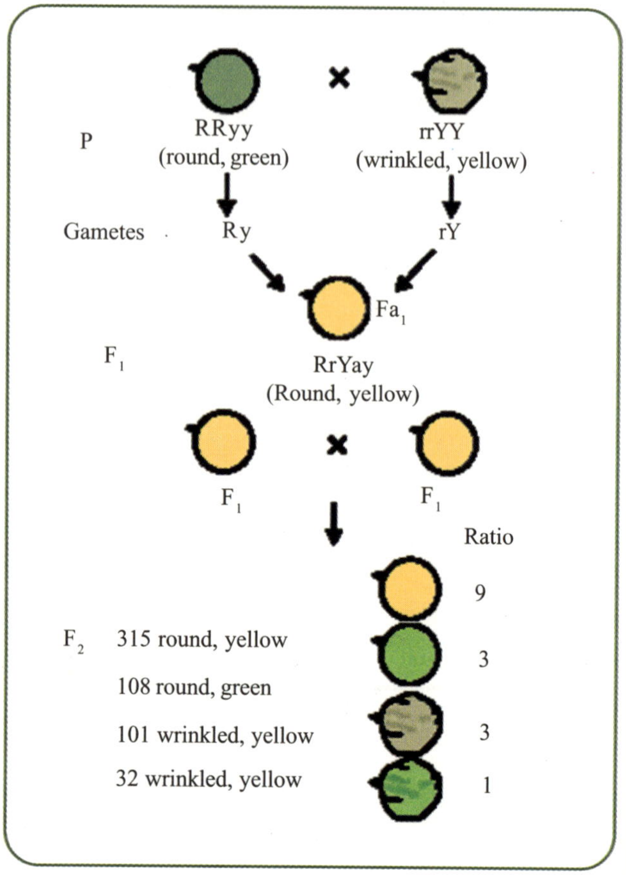

Independent inheritance of two separate traits. Shape and colour of seeds

- Roundness (R) and yellow colour (Y) are dominant characteristics, whereas wrinkled shape (r) and green colour (y) are recessive characteristics.
- The inheritance of these two characteristics is given below:

◆ In 1902 the experimental findings by **T. Boveri** and **W.S. Sutton** proved that gene is a part of chromosome. It was also found that the mode of transmission of chromosomes and genes (Mendel's 'factors') were strikingly similar. Also both genes and chromosomes are present in pairs.

◆ During meiosis in sexual reproduction each gamete formed contains unpaired gene or chromosome.

◆ When two gametes (male and female) unite after fertilization, the paired feature is restored in the zygote which eventually develops into an individual.

As a result continuity of life is maintained.

◆ After the discovery of chromosome it became evident that genes are located on the chromosomes at the fixed positions.

◆ Genes are many more in number than chromosomes because organisms have more characteristic features than the number of chromosomes. For example, in man the total number of chromosomes is 23 pairs but the total number of characters are 30,000 to 40,000.

Thus, genes of an individual are responsible for the characteristic features.

Questions

1. If a trait A exists in 10% of a population of an asexually reproducing species and a trait B exists in 60% of the same population, which is likely to have arisen earlier? (1 mark)
2. How do Mendel's experiments show that traits may be dominant or recessive? (2 marks)
3. How do Mendel's experiment show that traits are inherited independently? (3 marks)

Genes

◆ The genes that carry information from parents to offspring are segments of DNA.

◆ They are located on a chromosome occupying specific positions.

- The gene carries the specific sequence of nucleotides (genetic code) which enables cells to assemble amino acids in the correct order to make proteins. Hence, gene is a hereditary unit of a specific biological function.
- The nature of gene is responsible to maintain constancy through generations. However gene mutations occur when the sequence of bases is incorrectly copied during DNA replication causing variation. **Mutations are the sudden heritable changes.**
- Each gene set is present in a germ cell as separate independent pieces called chromosomes.
  - Each cell has two copies of each chromosome, one each from the two parents.
  - Every germ cell will take one chromosome from each pair and these may be of either maternal or paternal origin.
  - When two germ cells unite, they restore the specific number of chromosomes in the progeny.

Sex determination

- In a human cell there are 23 pairs of chromosomes.
- 22 pairs are described as **autosomes**.
- One pair which is found to be associated with sex determination is called **sex chromosome**.
- Females have two identical sex chromosomes designated as X and males have two different sex chromosomes designated as X and Y.
  - Females produces gametes with similar type of chromosomes. All the female gametes carry one X-chromosome, therefore they are **homogametic**.
  - 50 per cent of the male gametes carry X chromosome and 50 per cent carries Y chromosome. Therefore, males are **heterogametic**.
- The sex of the offspring is determined by the involvement of sex chromosomes during fertilization.

The diagram shows how a person's sex is inherited. **Notice** that:

- the sex of an offspring depends on whether the egg is fertilised by a sperm carrying an X chromosome or one carrying a Y chromosome.
- the birth of (almost) equal numbers of girls and boys is governed by the production of equal numbers of X and Y sperms at meiosis.

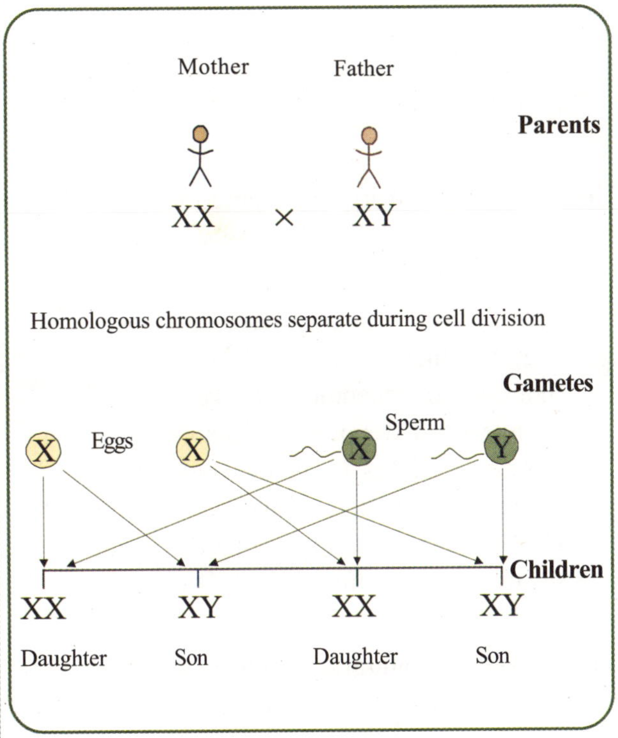

Inheritance of sex in humans

- Sometimes sex determination is regulated by environmental factors.
  - In some reptiles, the temperature at which the fertilized egg is incubated determines the sex.
  - In a turtle (*Chrysema picta*) high incubation temperature results in the development of female progeny.
  - In case of lizard (*Agama agama*), high incubation temperature gives rise to male progeny.

Questions

1. Define genetics. (2 marks)
2. Who is known as the "father of genetics"? (1 mark)
3. What is a sex chromosome? (1 mark)

Evolution

The classification of organisms put forward by Carolus Linnaeus (1707–1778) provided an insight to evolutionary relationship among the organisms.

- Present day living things have descended from ancestors that have changed through thousands of generations. This process of change is called evolution. Thus, evolution can also be defined as 'the gradual unfolding of organisms from pre-existing organisms through change since the beginning of life.' Evolution of the living organisms is called 'Organic Evolution.'

It is believed that natural selection among other processes, contributes to the evolution of new species and that the great variety of living organisms on the earth is the product of years of evolution including natural selection.

Example to understand evolution

Case I

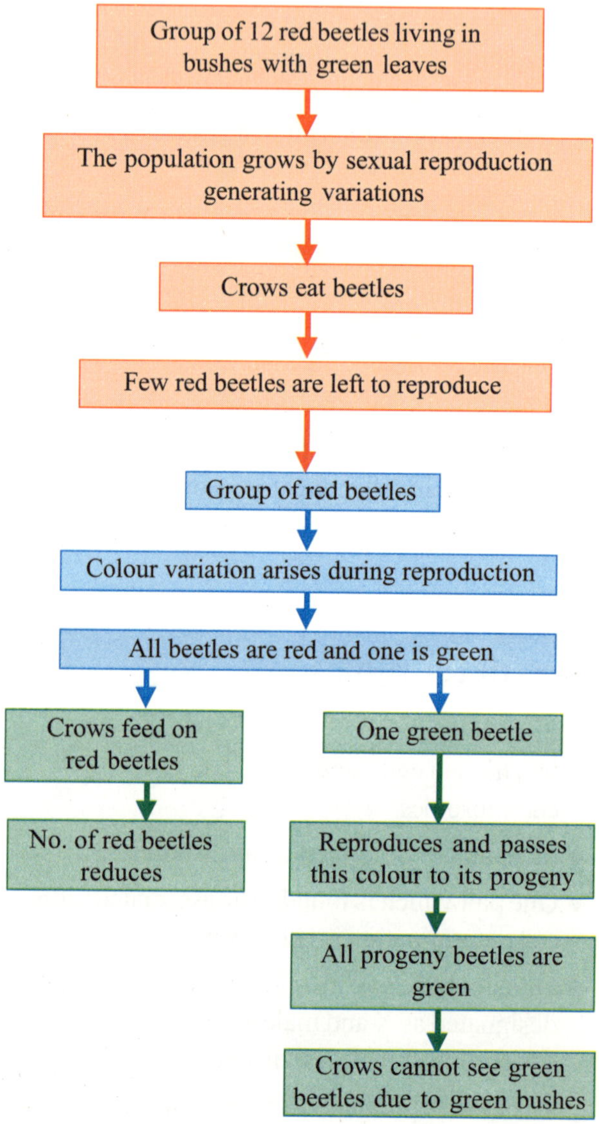

As a result there are more green beetles than the red ones

Case II

Group of red beetles
↓
Colour variation arises during reproduction. The beetle produced is blue in colour instead of red.
↓
One blue beetle reproduces and passes on the colour to its progeny
↓
Crow can see both red and blue beetles and eat them
↓
The population of both red and blue beetles decreases
↓
An elephant comes by and stamps on the bushes killing most of the beetles
↓
The few beetles that survived are blue
↓
Gradually the beetle population expands and the beetles are mostly blue

Let us now view all the cases.

Case I

- The variation (of green colour of the beetle) became common because it gave a survival advantage. Natural selection is observed in this case, which is actually affected by crows. Thus, adaptations in the beetle population, help to fit their environment better.

Case II

- There was no survival advantage to beetles by change of colour from red to blue. The common characteristic of the resultant population was changed later. Since the population of beetles was not large it was affected by the accident caused by elephant. Thus accident in a small population can change the freqency of some genes in a population, even if they give no survival advantage. Thus is called genetic drift which provides diversity without any adaptations.

Genetic drift is defined as the random changes in the gene frequency occurring by chance. The effect of genetic drift is very small in a large population but large in a small population.

Case III

Beetle population expands, bushes start suffering from a plant disease
↓
Amount of leaf material for the beetle is reduced
↓
Beetle are poorly nourished
↓
Average weight of adult beetles decreases
↓
No genetic change occurs
↓ After a few years
Plant disease is eliminated

Acquired and inherited traits

- As you know, the germ cells of sexually reproducing organisms are produced in reproductive tissue.
  - Any change that occurs in the non-reproductive tissue will not change the DNA of the germ cells. For example, in the case discussed earlier in the chapter, low weight of beetles caused due to starvation is not inherited over generations.
  - Thus, change in non-reproductive tissue cannot be passed on to the DNA of the germ cells. For example, if the tails of one group of mice are removed by surgery for three

consecutive generations, still tail-less progeny will not be produced; therefore evolution cannot be directed by removing tails.

- The removal of tail cannot change the genes of the germ cells of the mice.

◆ **Charles Robert Darwin** (1809–1882) was a keen British naturalist who abandoned medicine at Edinburgh and studied theology at Cambridge. His world voyage on HMS *Beagle* provided much of the evidence to suggest that:

- organisms evolve, and that
- natural selection is the mechanism of evolution.

It was another 20 years before he published these proposals in his book **Origin of species**.

Darwin explained that in spite of enormous potential of fertility, population size of any kind of organism remains limited. This is due to struggle between the members of the same species or different species for food, shelter and mate. The struggle leads to the survival of only superior ones (possessing favourable variations) and elimination of the unfit, weaker members. This is called **natural selection**. The variations of surviving species when get accumulated over a long period of time leads to the origin of a new species.

Darwinism was criticised as it could not explain how variations arise. The theory was then modified to synthetic theory of evolution which is based on the interaction of genetic variation and natural selection. This theory is most accepted now.

Questions

1. What is evolution? (2 marks)
2. Describe Darwin's theory of evolution. (2 marks)

Speciation

◆ Speciation is the process by which one species splits into two or more.

- For speciation to occur the populations should be isolated so that they do not interbreed to exchange genes.

The following check list of points refers to the concept map given on page 103.

Check List

1 ◆ Bushes on which the beetles feed are spread widely over a mountain range.

As a result, the beetle population becomes very large.

- The two populations of beetles are partly separated—one on the plains and the other on the mountains.
- Beetles do not travel far. So there are sub-populations in neighbourhoods.
- Most matings occur within these sub-populations.

2 ◆ Occasionally one beetle might go from one site to another.

◆ Then the migrant beetle will repoduce with the local population.

3 ◆ Genes of the migrant beetle will enter a new population.

- This is the gene flow occuring between populations that are partly, but not completely separated.

4 ◆ If a large river comes into existence between two partly separated sub-populations, the two populations get further isolated.

- Gene flow between the populations decreases further.

Let us now come back to the case of beetles again and study how speciation occurs.

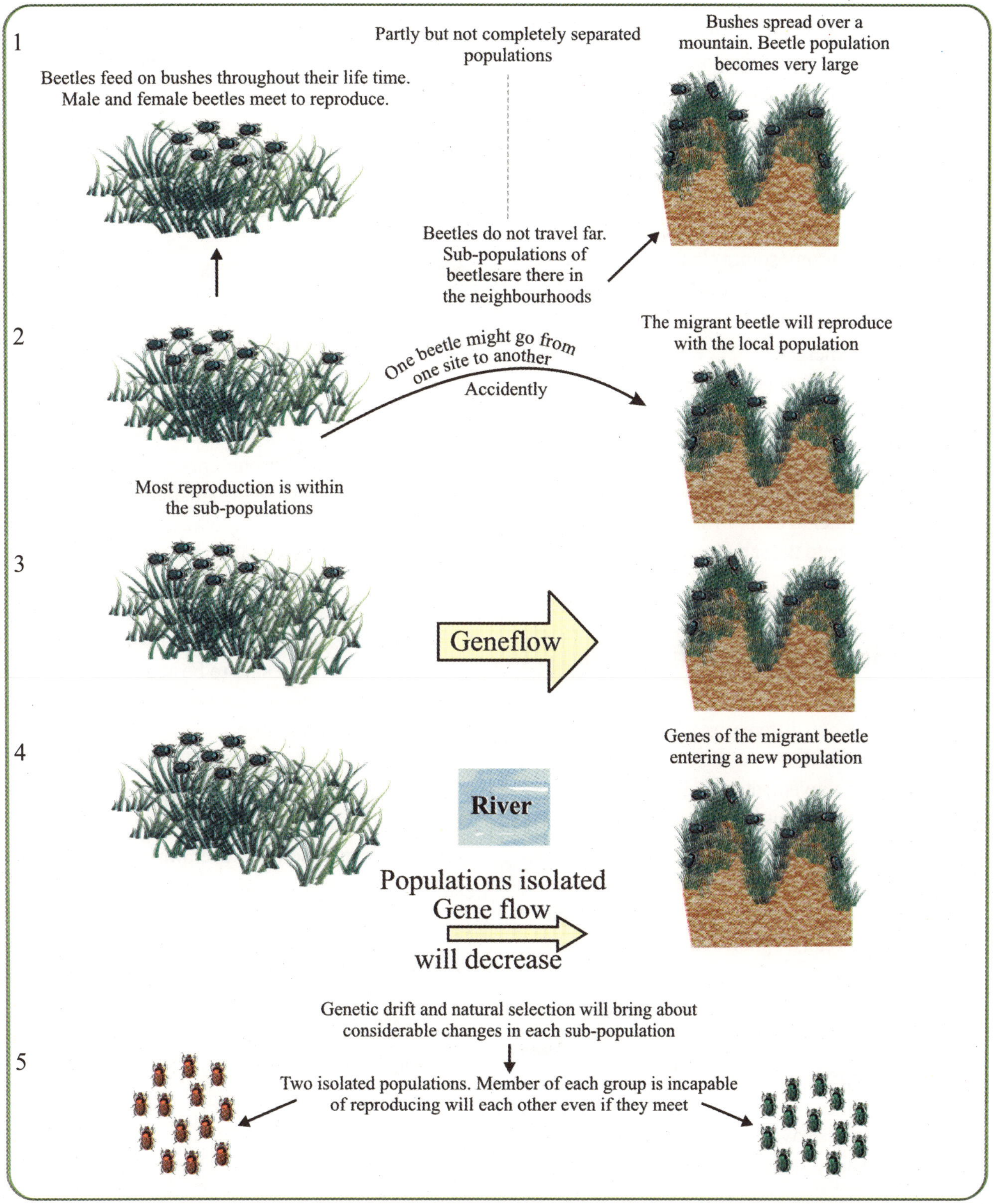

5 ◆ Over generations, genetic drift will accumulate different changes in each sub-population.

- Natural selection will also operate differently in the different geographic locations.

As a result, the two sub-populations will become incapable of reproducing with each other even if they happen to meet.

The genetic drift and natural selection will result when

(a) number of chromosomes changes in one of them so that the germ cells of the two groups cannot fuse with each other.

(b) due to the emergence of new variation, green females will not mate with red males.

Question

1. Why are human beings who look so different from each other in terms of size, colour and looks said to belong to the same species? (2 marks)

Evolution and classification

◆ Similarities and differences among organisms help us divide them into different groups so that it becomes convenient to study their characteristics. This is the basis of classification of living organisms.

- Characteristics are details of appearance or behaviour. For example, we have four limbs or plants can do photosynthesis is a characteristic.

◆ There are certain characteristics that are basic. For example, the cell is the basic unit of life in all organisms is a basic characteristic of all organisms.

◆ If two species have more characteristics in common, they are more closely related.

- The more closely the two species are related, the more recently they will have had a common ancestor.

◆ Species with recent common ancestors form a small group.

- These groups can further form super groups with more distant common ancestors.

Evolution by stages

◆ French biologist Jean Baptiste de Lamarck proposed the theory of **inheritance of acquired characters** or **Lamarckism**. The theory stated that organisms evolved because changes in the environment cause changes in the characteristics of organisms. The characteristics are said to be acquired and Lamarck believed them to be inherited by offspring. Variations that arise from environmental causes are not inherited because the sex cells are not affected. Instead the characteristics are said to be acquired. Lamarck explained the theory in his book, **Philosophie Zoologiue**.

Lamarck theory was disagreed by August Weismann who showed that even after cutting the tails of mice continuously for 21generations, a tail-less mouse was never born.

Let us consider a few examples:

Eye

◆ Both invertebrates (not all) and vertebrates have eyes.

- The structure of the eye in each of these organisms is different.
- This shows that they have separated during evolutionary changes.

Features

- It is quite possible that feathers could have formed for insulation and later used for the purpose of flight.
- Feathers were found in some dinosaurs but they were not used for flying.
- Later birds seem to have adapted and used the feathers for flying.
- This shows a close evolutionary relationship between birds and reptiles.

Wild cabbage plant

- Wild cabbage plant has been modified to different vegetables by artificial selection. Let us see how it has been done.
- If we focus on the idea that changes in DNA during reproduction are the basic events in evolution then comparing the DNAs of different species should give us a direct estimate of how much the DNA has changed during evolution of a species.
    - This type of study is known as **molecular phylogeny**.
    - It is based on the idea that organisms which are more closely related will have a greater degree of similarities in their DNA.

Evolution is different from progress.

- Evolution means generation of diversity and the adaptation of organisms according to their environmental needs.
- Progress means
    - One species need not get eliminated to give rise to new one.
    - The newly emerged species may be better than the older ones.
- Example—Human beings and chimpanzees have a common ancestor which is neither human nor chimpanzee.

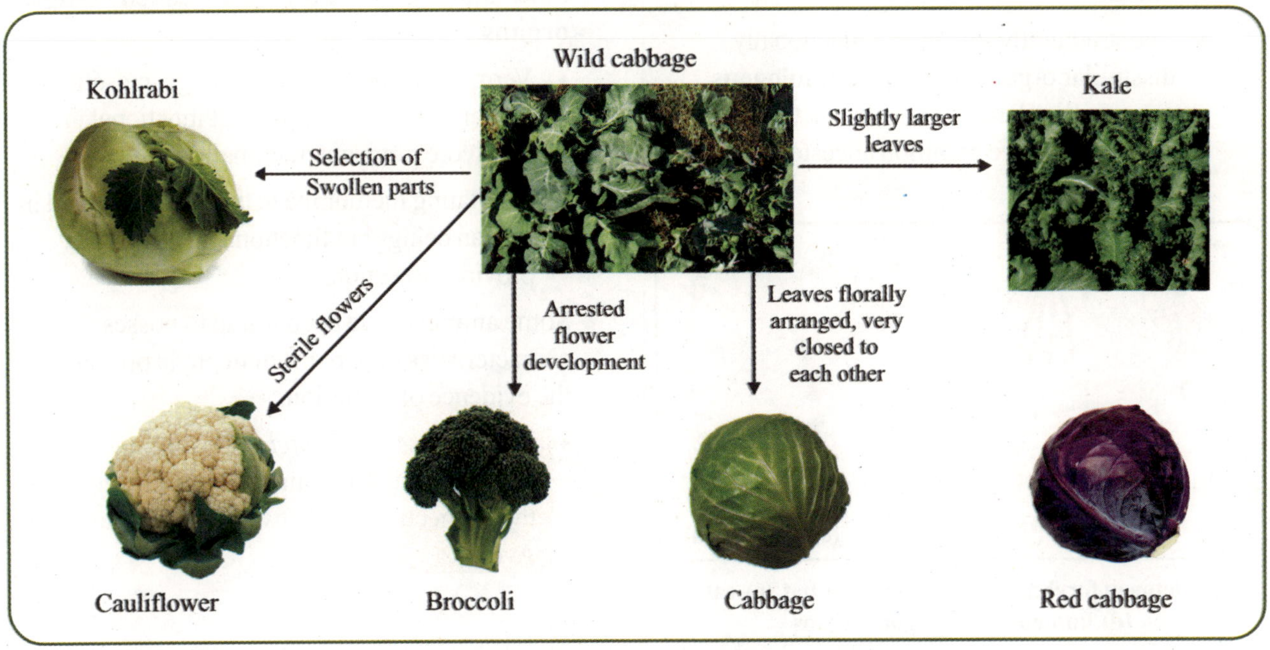

This is an evidence for evolutionary relationships

Human evolution

- The tools like excavating, time-dating, studying fossils, determining DNA sequences have been used for stydying human evolution.
- We all originated from Africa. The earliest members of the human species, *Homo sapiens* have been traced there.
    - Some of the humans left Africa to migrate slowly across the planet from Africa to West Asia, then to Central Asia, Eurasia, South Asia, East Asia.
    - This is yet another proof of evolution.

Tracing evolutionary relationships

A number of common features of different kinds of organisms provide evidences in favour of evolution.

- The forelimbs of man, cat, whale and bat develop in a similar fashion but have different functions.
    - The structurally similar and functionally dissimilar organs are called **homologous organs**. Similarities indicate that these vertebrates have common ancestors.

Skeleton of forelimbs of (a) whale (b) bat (c) cat (d) human—homologous organs

- The wings of a bird and a bat are developmentally and structurally very different but perform the same function. The bird wing is formed from skeleton, flesh and feathers whereas that of a bat is a fold of skin stretched mainly between elongated fingers.
    - The organs which are structurally different but perform the same function are called **analogous organs**.

Wings of (a) bird (b) bat—analogous organs

- Many organisms possess certain organs which are not functional but they are homologous with an organ that was functional in the ancestor or other animals. These organs are called **vestigial organs**.
    - Vermiform appendix of the large intestine in human beings is vestigial but functional in herbivore ruminant mammals.
    - Nictitating membrane in the eye is vestigial in human beings but functional in birds to provide protection.
- Some animals have been found to possess characteristics of two different phyla providing the evidence of evolution.
    - The fossil *Archaeopteryx* possesses characteristics of both birds and reptiles. It is the connecting link between Reptilia and Aves.

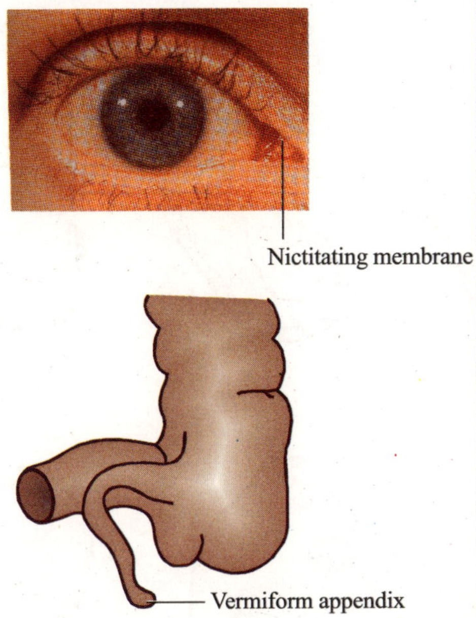

Vestigial organs in human body

Question

1. Name any three organs homologous to human hand. Why are they considered homologous? (3 marks)

Fossils

◆ Evolutionary relationships among various living organisms can be studied by fossils too.

- Fossils are the remains of animals and plants naturally preserved in various ways.

◆ The following explains how a fossil is formed.

- Suppose a fish living in a lake dies and gets embedded in mud or sand which was settling down on the bottom of a lake.
- After about 100 million years due to the pressure of more layers and change in the climatic conditions, the mud or sand turns into rock.
- Movements caused in earth may raise the rocks above water so that preserved skeletons can be found and chipped out of the rock.
- The deepest layers of rock are likely to contain the oldest fossils, and those closer to surface are recent. The second way of dating is by detecting the ratios of different isotopes of the same element in the fossil material.

Fact file

Ernst Haeckel (1834–1919) proposed **biogenetic law** which states that, 'ontogeny recapitulates phylogeny'. This means that during the embryonic development of any organism, its complete evolutionary history is repeated. In other words a comparative study of the different stages of the embryonic development of animals show that embryos are similar in early stages. This proves their common ancestry.

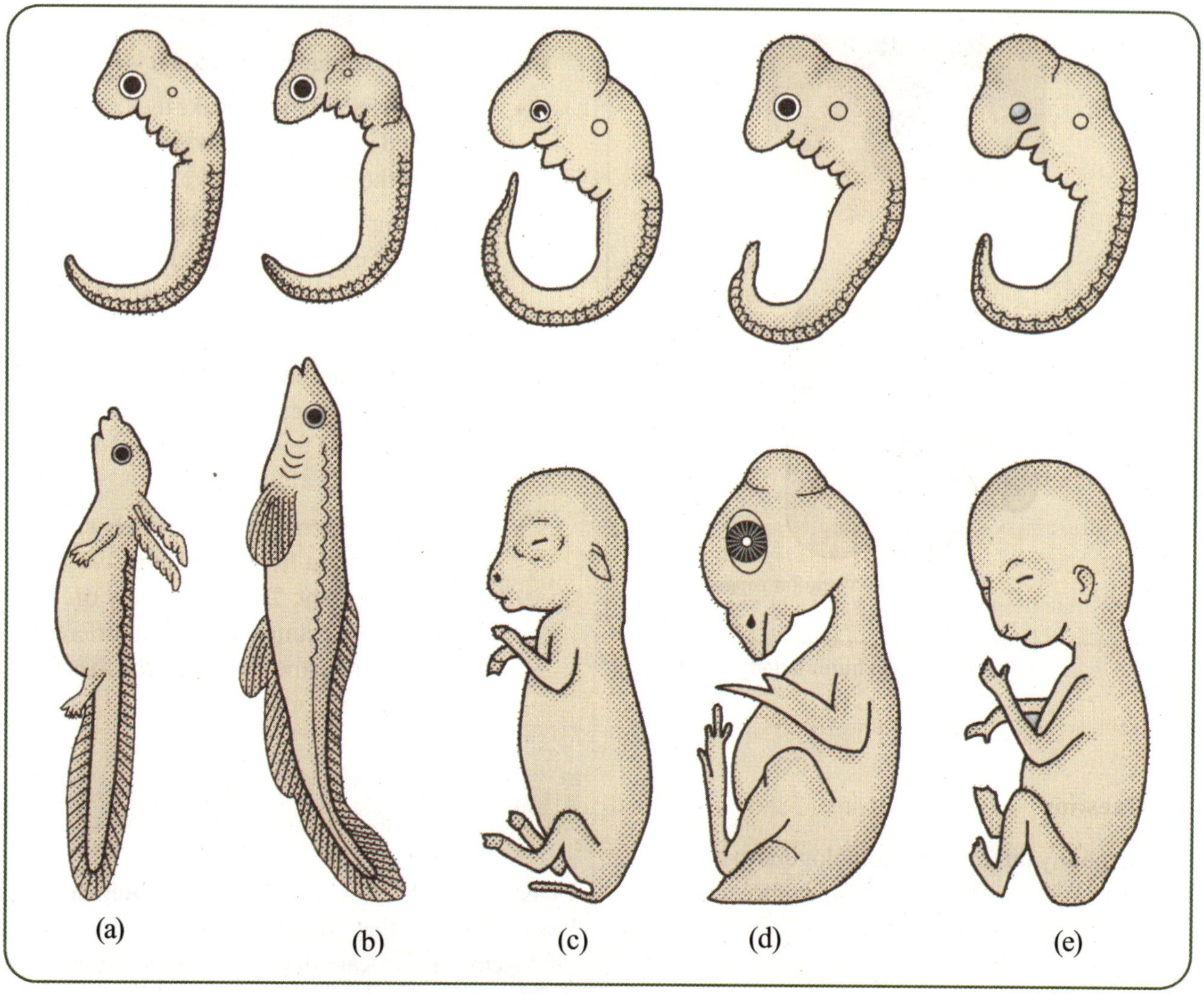

Comparison of both early and late stages of embryonic development of (a) salamander (b) fish (c) rabbit (d) chicken (e) human.

EXERCISES

I. Very Short Answer Questions

(1 mark)

1. Define the term 'evolution'.
2. What do you mean by variation?
3. Name the plant on which Mendel performed his experiments.
4. What is a chromosome?
5. What are Mendel's factors? What is the other term for it given by Johanssen?
6. How many chromosomes are there in a human (a) sperm and (b) liver cell?
7. The egg of an animal contains 11 chromosomes and out of them one is X-chromosome. How many autosomes would be there in its karyotype?
8. What are the components of a chromosome?
9. What do you mean by diploid set of chromosomes?
10. Define heredity.
11. Expand DNA and RNA.
12. Where are genes located and what is their chemical nature?
13. What are autosomes? How many autosomes are present in humans?
14. Why is a human male called heterogametic?
15. Where is a chromosome found?
16. Which of the two—sperm or ovum decides the sex of a child?
17. Why wings of a bird and that of an insect are not considered homologous?
18. Why two strands of DNA are complimentary to each other?
19. Who discarded Lamarck's theory of inheritance of acquired characters?
20. What do you mean by homologous organs?
21. How RNA is different from DNA?
22. Why do we call human female as homogametic?
23. Who is called the Father of Genetics?
24. Name the book written by Lamarck.
25. Define Biogenetic law.
26. Give one drawback of Darwin theory.
27. Which is the most accepted theory of evolution?
28. Define the term 'mutation'.
29. How is male progeny favoured in *Agama agama?*
30. Name the connecting link between Reptiles and Aves.
31. Which ancient Indian medical practitioner was aware of the concepts of genetics before the findings of Mendel?
32. Who was Charles Darwin?
33. Name an organism in which vermiform appendix is functional and the other in which it is vestigial.
34. Define analogous organs.
35. Who was the first scientist to isolate DNA?

II. Short Answer Questions

(2 marks)

1. Differentiate between heredity and variation.
2. Describe the chromosome structurally.
3. What are retroviruses? Name any one.
4. How do you differentiate between haploid and diploid chromosomes?
5. What is the significance of Karyotype?
6. Explain why in humans the sex of the child is determined by father and not by mother.
7. Differentiate between autosomes and sex chromosomes.
8. How are GMO produced?
9. Define the terms
   (a) homogametic
   (b) heterogametic.
10. Why is the study of fossils significant in the field of evolution?
11. How does Lamarckism promote the theory of 'use and disuse' of organs?
12. Why Lamarckism was strongly criticised by Weismann?
13. State Darwin's theory.
14. A married couple has four girl children but no boys. This does not mean that the husband produces only X sperms. Explain why not.
15. In terms of evolution, what is the importance of homology between a human hand and a wing of a bird?
16. Explain how analogous organs support the theory of organic evolution.
17. How do genes control traits?

III. Short Answer Questions

(3 marks)

1. Why organisms reproducing asexually show more hereditary features?
2. How do we come to conclusion that heredity and its concepts were known to the ancient civilisation?
3. Why did Mendel choose pea plant to work upon?
4. With suitable examples, discuss how temperature during incubation period affects sex determination in some animals.
5. With the help of a diagram, explain sex-determination in human beings.
6. What is the contribution of Mendel to Genetics?
7. What do you understand by 'struggle for existence'?
8. Differentiate between Lamarckism and Darwinism.
9. Explain the phrase 'Ontogeny recapitulates phylogeny'.
10. Justify that many genes are present on one chromosome.
11. How do homologous organs provide evidence of organic evolution?
12. Explain the terms
    (a) analogous organs (b) vestigial organs.

IV. Long Answer Questions

(5 marks)

1. Who is called the Father of Genetics? What were his contributions?

2. Explain how a gene, a DNA and a chromosome are structurally and functionally related to each other.
3. Discuss the morphological and anatomical evidences of evolution.
4. What are the main steps associated with the making of transgenic organisms?
5. Explain the 'Theory of Natural Selection' by Darwin. What was the drawback of his theory?
6. Giraffes acquired long necks and long front legs, after a prolonged period of evolution. Explain the process of evolution on the basis of Darwinism and Lamarckism.
7. What are fossils? How do the study of fossils support evidences for organic evolution?
8. What are vestigial organs? How do they support the fact that 'evolution has taken place'? Give some examples of vestigial organs.
9. How does embryology provide evidence for organic evolution?

TEST YOURSELF

Fill in the blanks

1. Mendel performed his experiment on ______ plant.
2. Genes are present on ______ at specific positions.
3. AIDS virus contains ______ as hereditary material.
4. Down's syndrome is caused due to the inheritance of an extra ______ chromosome.
5. The forelimbs of a bat and the hands of human being are ______ organs.
6. Lamarck's work was published in his book called ______.
7. Binomial system of nomenclature was given by ______.
8. When a sperm carrying X chromosome fertilises an egg, the zygote develops into ______.
9. A prokaryotic cell has ______ chromosome.
10. Viruses having RNA as genetic material are called ______.
11. There is/are ______ sex chromosome(s) in a human male.

Multiple-Choice Questions

Choose the correct option.

1. What is not true for a chromosome?
   (a) consists of two units called chromatids
   (b) contains a number of genes
   (c) DNA is their main constituent
   (d) they are never haploid

2. The chromosomes in a normal human female are represented by
   (a) 44 + XX (b) 44 + XY
   (c) 22 + XX (d) 22 + XY

3. The sex chromosomes in a human male are
   (a) one X chromosome
   (b) two Y chromosomes
   (c) one Y chromosome
   (d) one X and one Y chromosome

4. Wings of birds and insects are
   (a) homologous organs
   (b) analogous organs
   (c) vestigial organs
   (d) locomotory organs

5. Nictitating membrane in humans is an example of
   (a) homologous organ
   (b) analogous organ
   (c) vestigial organ
   (d) protective organ

6. The concept of origin of species by natural selection was given by
   (a) Lamarck (b) Weismann
   (c) Darwin (d) Charaka

7. Which among the following is a fossil that had both wings and teeth?
   (a) Snake (b) *Archaeopteryx*
   (c) Coucal (d) Equus

8. Who coined the term gene?
   (a) Morgan (b) Mendel
   (c) Johanssen (d) De Vries

9. The name of the book written by Charles Darwin is
   (a) Philosophie zoologique
   (b) The origin of species
   (c) Evolution of species
   (d) HMS Beagle

Answers to Multiple-Choice Questions

1. (d) 2. (a) 3. (d) 4. (b)
5. (c) 6. (c) 7. (b) 8. (c)
9. (b)

8 OUR ENVIRONMENT

The environment of an organism is its physical and biological surroundings with whom it interacts. Our environment is continuosly affected by activities of humans and natural processes. Human beings in their selfish interest have tried to modify the environment giving rise to environmental imbalance. It is important that we act judiciously and try to repair the damages done to the environment. Man will have to pay for every environmental change and disaster.

Environmental problems Imbalance in the environment leads to many problems like pollution, soil erosion leading to floods, depletion of natural resources, deforestation, landslides, change in the directions of rivers, extinction of species, waste accumulation and global warming.

Activity 1

To show that domestic waste can be biodegradable or non-biodegradable.

1. Collect all waste material generated in one day from your home.
2. Make a list of all waste things like empty cartons, vegetable peels, milk packets and waste paper.
3. Bury all the waste material in a pit in a nearby garden or in an old bucket containing at least 15 cm of soil.
4. Keep the content moist and observe two to three times after every 15 days.
5. Now match your list of waste things with those given in the following table and tick (✓) or cross (×) whatever is applicable.

Waste things	Spoilt food	Vegetable peels	Used tea leaves	empty milk polypack	empty cartons	waste paper	empty medicine bottles	empty medicine strips	old & torn clothes	old broken footwear
remains unchanged over a long period of time										
changes its form over time										
changes very fast										

Now choose the biodegradable and non-biodegradable substances from the list.

The kind of waste

- The food we eat is digested by various enzymes but the enzymes are specific in action. For example, the enzyme responsible for the digestion of proteins cannot digest carbohydrates.
- There are many materials in our surroundings which cannot be broken down by enzymes present in the living organism. For example, plastics cannot be broken down by the action of bacteria or other saprophytes. Such materials can be broken down by physical processes occuring at different conditions of temperature and pressure.
  - Substances like polymers persist in the environment for a very long time.

The waste material is grouped as biodegradable and non-biodegradable.

- **Biodegradable waste** is broken down by the activity of microorganisms into simpler and harmless products which enter into the biogeochemical cycles.
  - **Examples** are urine and faecal matter, sewage, domestic waste products, agricultural residue, paper, wood and cloth.
- **Non-biodegradable waste** cannot be broken down into simpler and harmless products. They also enter the food chain and harm the organisms in an ecosystem. These substances are inert.
  - **Examples** are insecticides, DDT, pesticides, arsenic, aluminium, plastics and radioactive waste.

Activity 2

1. Refer to books on the environment from the library or check the relevant resources available on internet to know more about biodegradable and non-biodegradable substances.
2. Find how long the non-biodegradable substances last in the environment.
3. Nowadays biodegradable plastics such as PHBV are available.
4. Find about some more biodegradable materials used in everyday life.

Ecosystem and its component

- The balance in nature is maintained by the interaction among plants, animals, microorganisms and human beings as well as with the physical surroundings.
- The **ecosystem** is formed of all the living organisms in an area together with the nonliving constituents.
  - For example, garden is an ecosystem.
- An ecosystem consists of **biotic** and **abiotic** components.
  - The biotic components include living organisms and abiotic components comprise physical factors like temperature, rainfall, wind, soil and minerals.
  - The growth and reproduction of the constituents of biotic component (i.e., living organism) in an ecosystem is affected by the abiotic components (i.e., non-living components) of that ecosystem.

The following chart will help you remember the components of ecosystems.

Ecosystem

Biotic (Living)	**Abiotic (Non-living)**
• Plant (Producers)	• Air
• Animals (Consumers)	• Soil
• Microorganisms (Decomposers)	• Water
	• Temperature
	• Humidity
	• Pressure

◆ The examples of natural ecosystems are forests, ponds and lakes.

◆ The example of man-made or artificial ecosystems are gardens and crop-fields.

Activity 3

1. Make a list of things which fish generally require for their survival.
2. The list will include fish food, oxygen, and water.
3. Drop some small aquatic plants and animals in the container and then drop some fish into it.
4. Install oxygen pump in the container to provide oxygen.
5. Clean this artificial ecosystem regularly.

◆ The living organisms which form the biotic component of an ecosystem can be classified into three groups.

◆ **Producers** include green plants and some blue green algae which prepare food in the presence of chlorophyll and sunlight by the process of photosynthesis. The food is in the form of compounds like sugar and starch.

- **Bacteria** and **fungi** are non-green plants.

◆ **Consumers** are the organisms that feed on plants.

- The organism that feed on plants directly are called the **primary consumers**.
- The primary consumers are fed upon by **secondary consumers**. In other words, the secondary consumers depend indirectly on the producers.
- Heterotrophs or consumers can be **herbivores** (plant eating) or **carnivores** (animal eating).

◆ **Saprophytes** derive their food from dead and decaying organisms ('sapro' means rotten).

- Saprophytes exhibit extracellular (outside the cell body) digestion. They release certain enzymes on the decaying matter (i.e., on which they grow) and convert complex food material into simple molecules. The simple soluble molecules are then absorbed by the organism.
- **Moulds, mushrooms** and **yeasts** are saprophytes.

◆ **Parasites** are organisms that live on or inside other organisms (called **hosts**) and obtain food from them without giving any benefit to them. They can be of two types:

- **ectoparasites** which live on the body surface of the host. For example, leech and head louse.
- **endoparasites** which live inside the body of a host. For example, hookworm, roundworm and tapeworm living in the intestine of man.
- Some plants like *Cuscuta* (amarbel) are parasites.
- Parasites have certain devices (body structures and skin) to obtain food from the host.

The significance of decomposers

- The decomposers which are bacteria and fungi, are most important in the decay process. They feed on the dead animals and plants or on their waste turning it back into simpler substances which then enters the soil.
  - The simpler substances enter the soil as mineral salts to be used up again by the plants.
  - Thus, decay process is important in the recycling of materials and it allows them to be used up again.
- In the absence of decomposers, all the materials will not be eventually returned to the environment and therefore some would run out.

Questions

1. What is meant by the term environment? (1 mark)
2. Name any two non-biodegradable wastes. (2 marks)
3. Name any two parasites. (2 marks)

Activity 4

In the previous activity we have discussed about designing an aquarium. If you recall, in the activity, it was mentioned to drop small aquatic animals in water. Now consider the following and write your views:

1. What if a large aquatic animal was dropped in water? What could have happened?

2. Write the aquatic organism in order of who eats whom and form a chain of at least three steps.

[ ] → [ ] → [ ]

3. Which group among the three would you consider to be of primary importance?

Food chains and webs

- Food chains show the feeding relationships and direction of energy transfer between a number of organisms.
- Each level of the food chain forms a trophic level.
  - The autotrophs or the producers are at the **first trophic level**. They fix the solar energy and make it available for consumers.
  - The herbivores or the primary consumers come at the **second trophic level**.
  - The small carnivores or the secondary consumers are at the **third trophic level**.
  - The larger carnivores or tertiary consumers form the **fourth trophic level**.
- All living things need energy to carry out their metabolic activities.
- The food we eat provides us energy to do work.
- The interactions among various components of the environment involves flow of energy from one component of the system to another.
- The autotrophs which are at the first trophic level capture solar energy and convert it into chemical energy.
  - This chemical energy supports the living world.
  - The energy is passed on from autotrophs to consumers (heterotrophs) and then to decomposers.
  - Each time the energy is passed on from one trophic level to the other, some of it is lost to the environment in forms which cannot be used again.

(a) (b) (c)

Food chain in nature: a) In a forest b) In a grassland c) In a pond

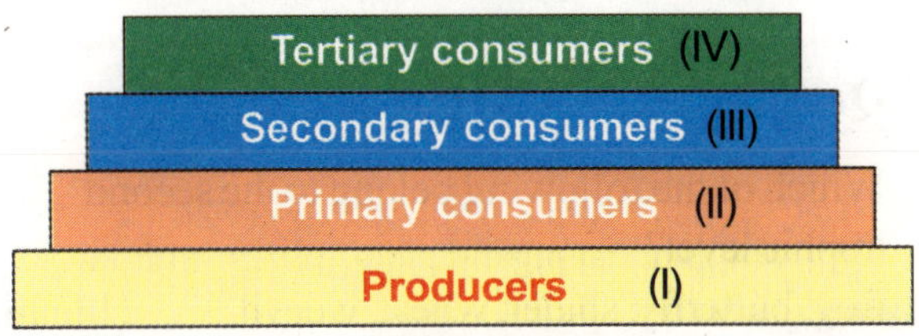

Trophic levels

- It is possible to produce pyramids by measuring the biomass in a food chain.
  - Biomass is the dry mass of the organism in a food chain.
  - The change in the size of the blocks from the base to the tip of a pyramid of biomass shows clearly the energy loss that occurs at each step.
- In a terrestrial ecosystem, green plants convert 1% of the total solar energy falling on them into food energy.
  - The primary consumers in the ecosystem feed on green plants. The energy contained in food goes to the primary consumer.
  - While the energy is transferred, from green plants to the primary consumers, a great deal of it is lost as

    a) heat to the environment.

    b) energy used in digestion and doing work.

    c) energy used in growth and reproduction.
  - The loss of energy at each step in the food chain (except the first step) is as much as 90%.
  - The biggest loss of energy in any food chain is between the sun and the producer.
- Thus an average of 10% energy is transferred at each step and reaches the next level of consumers.

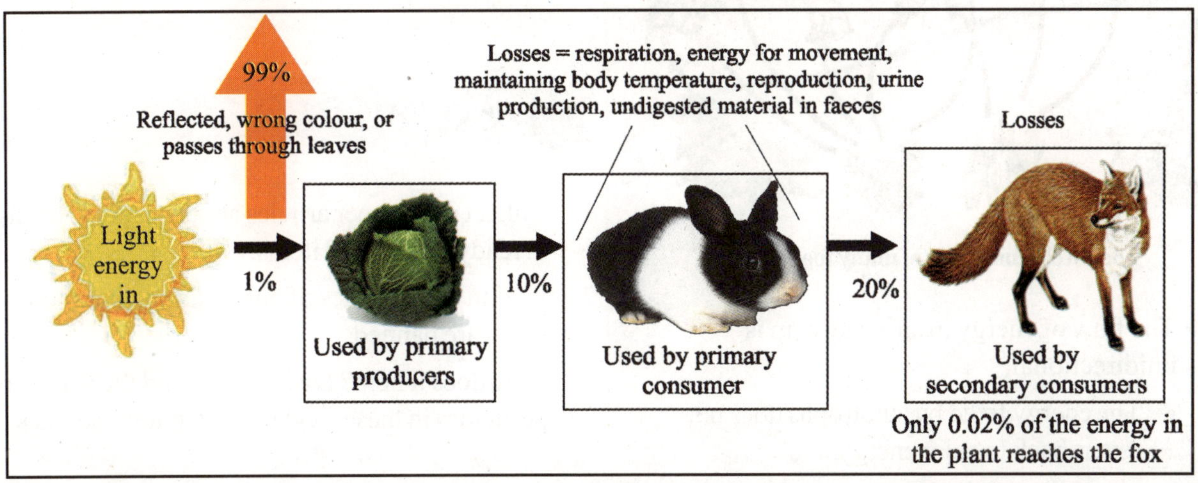

- As little energy is available at every consecutive step in a food chain, the food chains are small and they generally consist of only three or four steps.
  - Due to the loss of energy at each step, very little energy reaches the secondary and tertiary consumers.
  - This justifies a greater number of individuals at the lower trophic levels of an ecosystem. Thus, producers are largest in number.
- In nature consumers usually do not depend on only one type of food. As a result, food chains are interconnected at many points, forming a **food web**.

Food web, consisting of many food chains

- The flow of energy in an ecosystem is unidirectional.
  - The energy fixed by autotrophs does not revert back to solar energy.
  - Also the energy that passes on to primary consumer or herbivores from producers does not revert back to producers.
- When the energy moves progressively through various trophic level it is no longer available to the previous level.
- Not only energy but various harmful chemicals are also transferred through food chains.
  - For example, pesticides and fertilisers run-off from the land into rivers, lakes and the sea. These chemicals are also washed down into the soil.
  - The plants along with water and minerals absorb these chemicals from the soil.
  - The chemicals enter the body of aquatic plants and animals from water bodies.
  - Since the pesticides (chemicals) are non-biodegradable, these get accumulated at each tropic level.
  - This phenomenon is known as **biological magnification**.

Questions

1. Which of the following belong to the second trophic level?
   frog, butterfly, spider, wheat, weevil (1 mark)
2. Write a food chain in a forest ecosystem. (2 marks)

Activity 5

1. Collect newspaper articles about pesticide levels in ready-made food items.
2. Find in which states of our country these food items are banned.
3. How does it help? Discuss and find the source of pesticides in these food items. Could pesticides

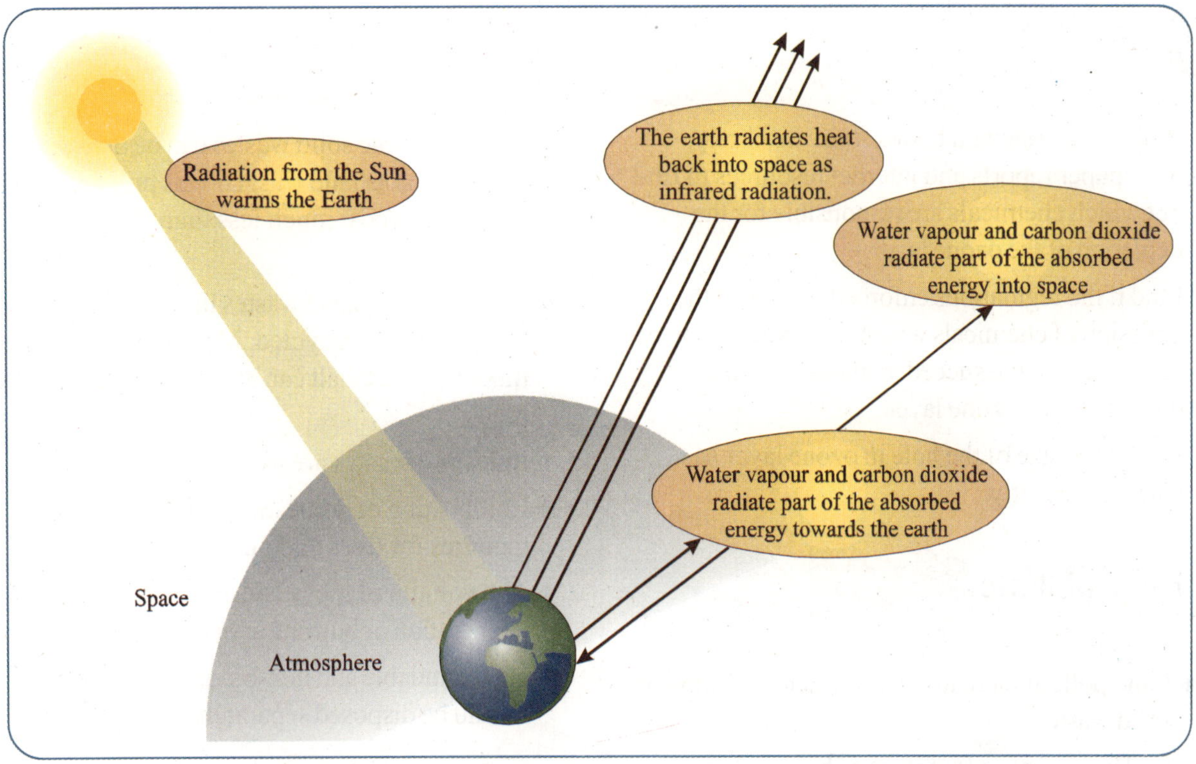

The greenhouse effect

get into our bodies from this source through other food products also?

4. Make a list of methods to be followed in order to avoid biological magnification.

Activities affecting the environment

- The human activities bring about changes in the environment.
- As we are an integral part of the environment, changes in the environment affect us.
- The two major environmental problems are depletion of the ozone layer and waste disposal.

Depletion of ozone layer

- Ozone (O_3) molecule constitutes three atoms of oxygen.
- Oxygen is important for survival of all aerobic life forms.
- Ozone is harmful for the living beings.
- When ultraviolet radiation acts on oxygen molecule up in the atmosphere, ozone is formed.

$$O_2 \xrightarrow{UV} O + O$$

$$O + O_2 \rightarrow O_3$$

- The higher energy radiations split apart some molecular oxygen into free oxygen atoms. These atoms then combine with the molecular oxygen to form ozone.

Activity 6

1. Refer to the relevant books from the library, newspaper reports and internet resources to find out which chemicals are responsible for the depletion of the ozone layer.
2. Find if the regulations enforced to control the emission of chemicals which lead to depletion of ozone layer have succeded in reducing the damage to the ozone layer.
3. Find if the size of the hole in ozone layer has changed recently.

Land pollution

- Land pollution is caused due to accumulation of solid waste.
  - The sources of wastes are houses, cattle shed, industries, agricultural fields.
  - Solid waste gets accumulated to form heaps which includes variety of things like fruits and vegetable peels, paper, clothes, plastics, ash, glass, leather, brick, metal and cow dung.
  - Chemicals like compounds of sulphur and lead eventually come to soil and pollute it.

Harmful effects

- The accumulation of waste threatens the health of people in residential areas.
- Waste decays and spreads foul smell, it encourages household pests and turns urban areas into dirty and unhealthy places to live in.
  - The waste may also block the water in the drain which becomes a breeding place for mosquitoes which are carriers of parasites causing malaria and dengue.

Modes of waste disposal

- Biodegradable solid wastes can be burried in urban areas as land fills. Biogas prepared from these waste cost much less than other fuel and fertilizers.
- Non-biodegradable wastes like plastics, metals and papers are recycled. Molten plastic waste mixed with asphalt can also be used for making roads.
- Industrial wastes are treated in special plants.
- Composting of domestic waste prepares manures for trees and plants.
- The volume of the waste can be reduced by incineration or burning at high temperature.
- Biodegradable and non-biodegradable waste should be disposed separately.

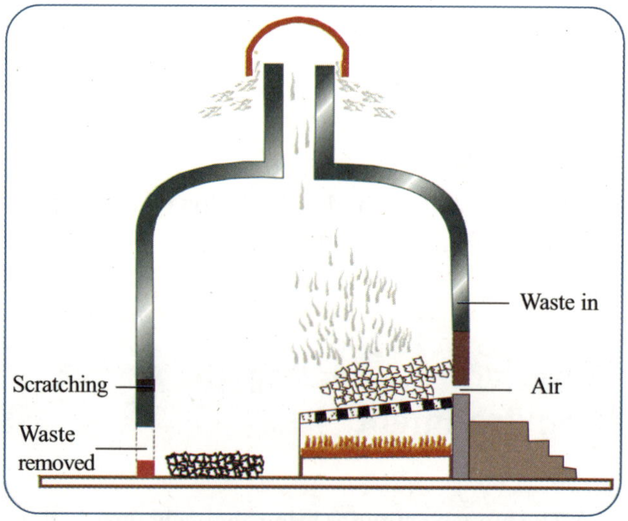

Incinerator

Activity 7

1. Try to find what happens to the waste generated at home.

2. Find if there are any means to collect the biodegradable and non-biodegradable wastes separately.

Activity 8

1. Make two separate lists one of waste generated at home in a day and the other of waste generated in your classroom in a day.
2. Find the percentage amount of biodegradable and non-biodegradable waste.
3. Make a list of ways to deal with both kinds of waste.

Water pollution

Water is said to be polluted when there is any physical, biological or chemical change in water quality that is harmful to humans and other organisms.

> ☞ **Remember** that potable or drinking water is one which
> * is transparent, colourless and odourless
> * is free from harmful substances and coliform bacteria
> * contains sufficient dissolved oxygen.

- ◆ **Some sources** of water pollution are those situated close to the water source. For example, factories, coal mines, oil wells and power plants. Factories need water to dispose off wastes. In case of all such sources of water pollution, it is possible to treat the waste before it enters the water body.
- ◆ **Some sources** of water pollution are scattered and generally not located near the water body. Pollutants from them eventually reach the water body. For example, pesticides. People produce sewage which (treated and untreated) enters rivers and the sea.

Activity 9

1. Find how the sewage in your locality is treated.
2. Find how the local industries in your locality treat their waste.

Activity 10

1. Find about disposing of electronic items. If not disposed properly, how would these materials affect the envionment?
2. Make a project file on recycling of materials.

Questions

1. Describe any two modes of disposal of waste. (3 marks)
2. Why we say energy flow in the biosphere is unidirectional? (2 marks)
3. What is biological magnification? (2 marks)

Conservation and protection of environment

Conservation is the maintenance of environmental quality and resources. It differs from preservation, which is considered to be maintaining of nature as it is, or might have been before the intervention of either human beings or natural sources.

Following practices help to conserve environment:

- use renewable resources in sustainable way and reduce the exploitation of nonrenewable resources through recycling and the use of alternative materials for the production of goods.
- use land in a way so that conflicting interests between human needs and the impact of these needs on the survival of wildlife and their environments are reduced.
- reduce pollution by treating sewage and developing more efficient industrial processes, which produce less waste and use less energy, and the introduction of more environment friendly methods of farming.
- establish **National Parks** to conserve areas of outstanding beauty and scientific interest.
- harvesting rain water and planting trees in place of those removed for various purposes.
- composting organic solid waste for use as manure.

◆ **Depletion of ozone layer** is caused by chlorofluorocarbons (CFCs). The CFCs are compounds used in refrigeration and fire extinguishers and as propellants in aerosols. They escape and react with ozone in the upper atmosphere. Oxygen is produced and the ozone layer which protects life on the earth from the harmful effects of ultraviolet radiation is gradually destroyed. Ultraviolet radiation causes skin cancer, damage to eyes and immune system. It also causes ecological disturbances, variations in global rainfall and decrease in food production.

◆ The earth receives radiation from the sun, and also radiates heat into space. Carbon dioxide and water vapour reduce the escape of heat energy from the earth by means of the **greenhouse effect**.

The combustion of fossil fuels is causing an increase in the level of carbon dioxide at a rate which could raise the average temperature of the earth. One result would be that the glaciers and the massive ice caps of the Arctic and Antarctic regions would slowly begin to melt. The levels of oceans would rise, and coastal areas would be flooded. Apart from carbon dioxide the other greenhouse gases are methane, chlorofluorocarbons (CFCs), nitrogen oxides and ozone.

Occupational hazards

There are certain occupations where workers are exposed to certain substances and agents (due to constant use of certain chemicals). These agents when enter their body (mostly by inhalation) lead to various disorders. Some of the common occupational diseases are tabulated below.

Disease	Symptoms	Causative agent	Occupation
Silicosis (or silico tuberculosis)	Chronic cough and pain in the chest	free silica or silicon dioxide	Working in ceramics and glass factories
Asbestosis	Cancer	Asbestos	Making ceilings
Byssinosis	Lung disease chronic cough and bronchitis	Cotton fibres	Cotton industry
Pneumoconiosis	Lung problems	Coal dust	Coal mining

Prevention and control

Techniques employed for controlling **gaseous pollutants**.

- **Scrubbers** are used in the chimneys of power stations. They remove sulphur from the waste gases produced by burning coal, before the gases escape into the atmosphere. Practically speaking, scrubbers are solvents which absorb pollutants from the gaseous effluents usually by dissolving them in itself.
- The gaseous effluents from the industries are passed through porous solid adsorbents kept in containers. The harmful particles are trapped at the surface of the solid adsorbent.
- When the pollutants are in the form of organic gases or vapours, they are converted into water vapour and relatively less harmful products, such as CO_2 by combustion or catalytic processes.

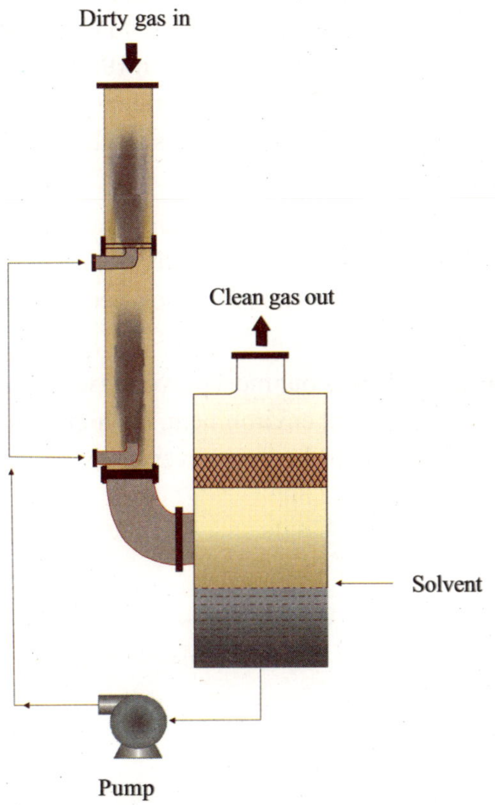

Reverse jet scrubber

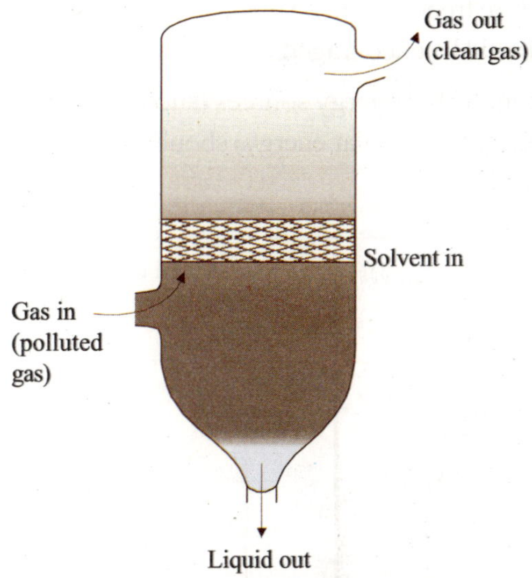

Wet scrubber

Techniques employed for controlling **particulate pollutants**.

- In case of particulate emissions, the particles can be made to settle down by gravitational force in **gravity settling chambers**. A sudden change in the direction of the gas flow also causes the particles to separate out.
- Gases containing particulate matter are passed through porous **fabric filters**. The particles present in the gas are trapped and collected in the filters.
- Particles from a gas stream may be removed by applying electric field (by virtue of their behaviour in an electrical field). When the gas is passed through electrodes, the particulate matter separates out by getting attracted to electrodes. Such devices are called **electrostatic precipitators**.
- Automobiles should adhere to emission control standards—**Bharat II** or **Euro II**.
- Industries and refineries should not be located in or near residential areas. They should adopt waste control measures.

◆ More trees should be planted and forestation should be encouraged.

◆ Renewable energy sources (such as wind, ocean currents and solar energy) should fulfill energy needs.

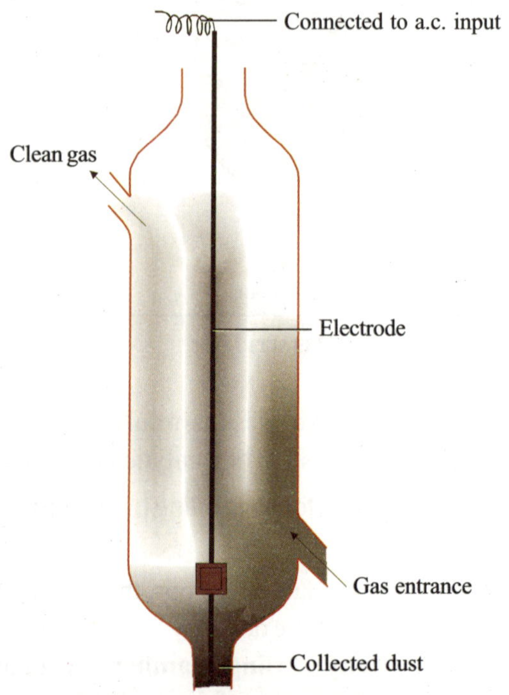

Electrostatic precipitator

◆ Better designed equipments, smokeless fuels, and hearths in industries and at home should be used. Also tall chimneys should be installed for vertical dispersion of pollutants.

Environmental laws

Some of the Indian laws to conserve and protect the environment are mentioned here.

- Prevention of Cruelty to Animals Act, 1960.
- Air (Prevention and Control of Pollution) Act 1981.
- Environment (Protection) Act 1986.
- Forest (Conservation) Act, 1980.
- Water (Prevention and Control of Pollution) Act, 1974.
- Wildlife (Protection) Act, 1972, amended in 1991.
- The Motor Vehicle Act, 1938, amended in 1988.

UNESCO sponsored, the International Union for Conservation of Nature and Natural Resources (IUCN) was established in 1948. Its 10th general assembly was held in New Delhi in 1969. The year 1972 was declared as the International year of Nature Conservation. Its main task is the practical implementation of laws.

The IUCN lists a variety of species that seem to touch the thin red line. These include one-horned rhinoceros, elephants and the black-necked crane to name some.

An aware citizen is our most powerful weapon in the battle to protect our environment. It's high time that nature conservation becomes everybody's concern.

EXERCISES

I. Very Short Answer Questions

(1 mark)

1. Define pollution.
2. What are pollutants?
3. Name two natural sources of air pollution.
4. What are fabric filters?
5. Name two mechanical devices used to control particulate emission.
6. What is oil slick?
7. Which chemicals are responsible for the infiltration of ultraviolet rays on the earth?
8. Write two conservation practices.
9. Define soil erosion.
10. What do you mean by deforestation?
11. Name the gas which causes greenhouse effect.
12. What are the sources of water pollution?
13. Write full form of CFC.
14. Define greenhouse effect.
15. Why are tall chimneys recommended for factories?
16. How quantity of waste on land can be reduced?
17. What do you mean by potable water?
18. Which of the following are biodegradable pollutants: DDT, urine, paper, plastic, sewage?
19. Which is environment friendly—paper or plastic?
20. What could be the cause of gradual increase in the atmospheric temperature?
21. Rearrange the following according to their trophic levels in a food chain: fish, zooplankton, seal, phytoplankton.
22. Name a pollutant which can enter into the human body through the food chain.
23. State one difference between autotrophs and heterotrophs.
24. Name one substance which damages the ozone layer.
25. What do you mean by occupational diseases?
26. Which disease can be caused due to prolonged inhalation of cotton fibres?
27. What do Bharat II or Euro II stand for?
28. Name some solid wastes.
29. Which of the following are water-borne diseases: cholera, jaundice, arthritis, typhoid?
30. What is a decomposer?
31. What is 'incineration'?
32. Which pollutant has the capacity to absorb infrared radiations?
33. Suggest one constructive way of dealing with plastic wastes.
34. Define environment.
35. Which one of the following is not a part of biotic environment: man, soil, ferns, reptiles?
36. Define conservation.

37. What is the need to enforce environment laws?
38. What is the commonest problem anticipated in the coal mine workers?
39. Define an ecosystem.
40. Name any two wastes that can be recycled and reused.
41. Define trophic level.
42. Define the term bioaccumulation.

II. Short Answer Questions

(2 marks)

1. Suggest two methods for water purification.
2. Give two reasons why heaps of solid wastes are a nuisance.
3. Give full form of CFCs. Name any three sources of CFCs.
4. What are the distinct characteristics of potable water?
5. How do industries contribute to the problem of water pollution?
6. Mention any two steps for sustainable development.
7. What is the impact of technological revolution on natural resources and the environment?
8. What is eutrophication? Mention its harmful effects.
9. Elaborate 'Industrialisation is one of the main cause of deterioration of environment'.
10. How a balance between CO_2 and O_2 is maintained in nature?
11. What is the role of decomposers in the environment?
12. Draw a schematic diagram of a food web.
13. How do food chains get shortened? How this affects the biosphere?
14. Explain how environment will be affected if all decomposers are removed.
15. Which food chains are advantageous in terms of energy?
16. Differentiate between a food chain and a food web.
17. Write a short note on CFCs.
18. Explain ten per cent law.

III. Short Answer Questions

(3 marks)

1. How activities of man affect nature?
2. How biodegradable substances work as pollutants?
3. List four probable sites from which there can be a run-off causing water pollution.
4. 'Excessive use of pesticides protects the crops but causes long term damage to the mankind.' Justify.
5. What do you mean by replenishment of natural resources?
6. What would be the effect if forests get depleted?
7. How does recycling of waste materials helps in maintaining ecological balance?
8. Give three examples to substantiate that man has misused natural resources to promote self-interest.
9. Due to urbanization there is an increase in the demand for paper in the last few years. How has it affected the environment?
10. With the help of an example, involving four organisms, describe how energy flows from different trophic levels.
11. Distinguish between biodegradable pollutants and non-biodegradable pollutants.

12. Describe a food chain found in a grassland. Give a digrammatic representation to support your answer.

IV. Long Answer Questions

(5 marks)

1. Discuss replenishment of the natural resources.
2. What is the significance of the environmental laws?
3. List five solid wastes and briefly explain how they cause soil pollution.
4. How can you make a balance between the environment and the development?
5. Write a note on sustainable development.
6. Write down the five effective ecofriendly steps that will help safeguard our environment.
7. What are the three major types of pollution? Name two pollutants of each type.
8. What are the main biosphere reserves in our country?

TEST YOURSELF

Fill in the blanks

1. Dead decomposed organic matter is called ______.
2. The agents that cause pollution are ______.
3. CFC's are used in ______ and ______.
4. ______ and ______ are known as green house gases.
5. Pollutants which can be easily broken down by the action of microorganisms are ______.
6. Depletion of ______ layer causes variation in global rainfalls.
7. ______ is the maintenance of environmental quality and resources whereas ______ is maintaining of nature as it is.
8. 1972 was declared as the International Year of ______.

Multiple-Choice Questions

Choose the correct option.

1. Ozone depletion has resulted in
   (a) warming of the Earth
   (b) less UV radiation on Earth
   (c) decrease in temperature
   (d) more UV radiation on Earth

2. Harmful UV radiations cause
   (a) fever (b) inflammation of liver
   (c) skin cancer (d) nausea

3. CFC's cause
   (a) depletion of ozone layer
   (b) depletion of CO_2
   (c) increase in ozone layer
   (d) increase of CO_2

4. Which among the following is a part of an aquatic ecosystem?
   (a) snake (b) crustacean
   (c) bat (d) grasshopper

5. The green house gases
   (a) keep the planet warm
   (b) decrease the temperature
   (c) radiate the heat of the earth
   (d) trap the harmful rays

6. The inhalation of cotton fibres over a long period of time causes
   (a) silicosis (b) asbestosis
   (c) byssinosis (d) pneumoconiosis

7. In the following food chain 1 J of energy is available to lion. How much energy was available at producer level?
   Producer → Deer → Lion
   1 J
   (a) 10 J (b) 1000 J
   (c) 100 J (d) 10,000 J

Answers to Multiple-Choice Questions

1. (d) 2. (c) 3. (a) 4. (b)
5. (a) 6. (c) 7. (c)

9 MANAGEMENT OF NATURAL RESOURCES

Management of natural resources

◆ Soil, air and water are the three main natural resources given to us by nature. Though these are renewable sources, they are getting highly polluted due to human activities.

◆ Similarly other natural resources like forests, wildlife, water, coal and petroleum are being overused by ever increasing population. These have to be managed and used judicially for sustainable development.

◆ At a global level there are alarming environmental problems. International and national laws are being formulated to help protect environment. Various national and international organizations are working to save the environment.

◆ This awareness about environmental problem has gained momentum in recent years as there is shortage of water, electricity and other resources in many parts of the world. Also there are changes in climate and weather patterns.

◆ Due to this awareness, government of India had started Ganga Action Plan in 1985. The objective of this multi-crore project was to improve the quality of water of Ganga. During the 2500 km course of Ganga from Gangotri to Ganga Sagar in Bay of Bengal, it turns from a life-giving river to a drain. Various cities and towns in Uttar Pradesh, Bihar, and West Bengal release their garbage, excreta and industrial waste into the Ganga.

- In addition to this people living on its banks carry out various human activities like bathing, washing, immersion of religious materials and ashes.

  As a result, the water of Ganga gets highly polluted and all fish get killed in large sections of the river.

Activity 1

1. Take a pH paper and collect a sample of water supplied in your locality.
2. Check the pH of water sample.
3. Check the pH of the water in the local water body (pond, river, lake, stream, etc.).
4. Does your observation predict about the purity of water?

◆ We all need to take action towards protection of environment and conservation of resources. Even small things can make a difference. You must have heard about three R's to save the environment: Reduce, Recycle and Reuse.

Reduce: This means cutting down on usage of resources like electricity, water and food. During day time lights need not be switched on. Water should not be used excessively; instead of shower, use bucket to take bath. Leaking taps should be repaired immediately. Food should not be wasted.

Recycle: This means that used plastic, metal paper and glass can be collected and recycled into required things rather than making fresh plastic, glass and paper etc. To do this, the garbage needs to be segregated so that these things which can be recycled do not mix with other waste.

Reuse: This is even better than recycle. Reuse means using a thing again and again rather than use once and throw. For example, a polythene can be used many times. Plastic and glass bottles and jars in which we get packaged foods can be collected and used in many other useful ways.

- The various chores we do in our daily routine can directly or indirectly affect our environment. So we have to be conscious of our decision. Our everyday choices can have immediate or long term effect on our environment.
- **Sustainable development** refers to growth with preservation of resources. We need to produce more and grow technically to meet our human needs but at the same time we have to preserve our environment for future generations.
  - Hence economic and scientific development is linked to environmental conservation.
  - Thus sustainable development implies a change in all aspects of life. And it depends upon people's willingness to change themselves to save environment.

Need to manage resources

- All the things we need to survive—food, water, shelter, clothes, books, toys etc., are made from the resources of mother Earth.
- Sun provides us energy which is transformed by organisms on Earth by various physical and chemical processes.
- The resources of Earth are not unlimited. But the demand for these resources is increasing exponentially due to ever increasing population of the world.
  - Hence we need to manage these resources in such a way that they will last for future generations. These should not be exploited for short term gains.
- All people irrespective of being rich or poor should have access to these resources.
- As we exploit natural resources we cause damage to the environment. For example, extraction of metals produces huge amounts of slag which is disposed carelessly.
- Sustainable natural resource development requires that we plan and dispose these wastes safely.

Forests and wildlife

- Forests play a very important role in economic growth of a country.
- Forests are called 'biodiversity hot spots'.
  - Biodiversity refers to the number of species found in an area.
  - These include different life forms such as bacteria, fungi, ferns, flowering plants, insects, nematodes, birds, reptiles, etc.
- This biodiversity of a region plays a very important role in ecological balance and hence needs to be conserved at any cost.
- Forests cater to our needs in different ways. Following are the people who directly depend on forests.
- **People living in or around forest** They depend on forests for firewood, timber, food materials etc.
  - Wood is needed to make tools for agriculture, fishing and hunting.

- Bamboo is used for making huts, baskets, mattresses etc.
- People gather fruits, nuts and medicines from the forests.
- Their cattle graze in forest area.

◆ **Industrialists** Various industries depend upon forests for raw materials. For example, bidi industry needs 'tendu' leaves.

- Paper mills need the raw material from forests.
- Timber industry needs wood from forest and sports equipments are made from wood.

◆ These industries do not take any step towards conserving resources. Industrialists lobby with the government officials to get access to forests at low prices. Once they get all possible raw materials (trees) from a forest, they move to a new area. They are not accountable for sustainability of forests so that the future generations also get their share of the forest resources.

◆ Before the British came to India, people had been living near forests for centuries. They followed practices which ensured sustainable use of forest. After the British took control of forest areas, they exploited the forests ruthlessly. They restricted local people to very small area and so the forests started getting over exploited. After the British, the forest department took over but they did not give importance to local people's knowledge and their needs.

As a result, large areas of forests were converted into monocultures of pines, teak or Eucalyptus. Planting of these monocultures required the areas to be cleared off, thus destroying the biodiversity of the area.

◆ **Wildlife and nature enthusiasts** They are the people who want to conserve the forest and have a say in their management. They began with big animals like lions, tigers and rhinoceros. Gradually they realized that biodiversity as a whole needs to be preserved.

◆ Nature enthusiasts do not include local people and their practices in their drive to conserve forests. Local people are known to work traditionally for conservation of forests. For example, Bishoi community in Rajasthan conserved the forests and wildlife as a religious tenet.

- Amrita Devi Bishnoi and 363 other people sacrificed their lives in 1731, to save the 'khejri' trees in khejrali village near Jodhpur. In her memory the Government of India has instituted 'Amrita Devi Bishnoi' National Award for wildlife conservation.

◆ The great Himalayan National park contains alpine meadows which were once grazed by sheep in summers. Nomadic shepherds brought their sheep there for grazing. Since the formation of park, this practice was stopped. Now, without any sheep to eat it, the grass grows very tall and then falls down, preventing fresh grass from growing.

◆ Keeping local people out of the management of protected area will not be possible in the long run. More than the local people, the damage is caused by outside agencies viz.,

i) Industries	– deforestation
ii) Building dams and roads	– cutting trees
iii) Tourists and their staying	– cause pollution due to arrangements made for their convenience

◆ Forest resources should be used in such a manner that it leads to development but does not harm the environment. The benefits of these resources should go to local people. Also a process should be followed in which decentralized economic growth and ecological conservation both are taken care of.

◆ The methods we choose to use these resources will determine whether the resources will be conserved or destroyed in future. We have to use these resources very carefully for our social and economic growth.

Sustainable management

- All the stakeholders should have common goal towards sustainable management of the forests.
- The 'Chipko Andolan' (Hug the trees movement) was the result of a grass root level effort to end the alienation of people from their forests. In 1970 in an incident in a remote village called Reni in Garhwal (Himalayas) a contractor was allowed to cut trees. However, he had a dispute with local people. One day when the village men were not around, the contractor and his workers came to cut the trees. To save the trees, the women of the village reached the forest and clasped the tree trunks, preventing workers from cutting them. Eventually the contractor had to go back.
- This Chipko movement quickly spread across the communities and media, forcing government to change its strategy about the use of forests.
- Local people do not cut the trees, they only pluck leaves and cut branches, leaving the tree to grow again over time. They realise that cutting trees affects quality of soil and water.
- Another example of people's participation in management of forests was in West Bengal. In 1972, the West Bengal forest department accepted its failure to protect Sal forests in the south western districts of the state. Due to traditional methods of policing and surveillance local people were completely alienated from the forests.

  As a result, various Naxalite led militant-peasant movements rose resulting in clashes between forest officers and villagers.

  - Then the department started a new project. In Arabari forest range of Midnapore district forest officer, A.K. Banerjee, involved villagers to protect 1272 hectares of damaged *Sal* forest. In return the villagers were given employment in silviculture and harvesting operations, 25 per cent of the final harvest and were allowed to collect firewood and fodder on paying a nominal fee.

    As a result of this effort, the forest recovered and was valued at Rs. 12.5 crores in 1983.

Questions

1. What do you understand by forest conservation? (1 mark)
2. What is sustainable development? (2 marks)

Water for all

- Water is essential to life. We have studied about the water cycle in previous classes. We are also aware how human activities are polluting water bodies. Not only this, human intervention also affects availability of water in various regions.
- Various regions in India depend upon monsoons for water. Most of the rains fall in certain months of the year. But due to the loss of vegetation cover, this water is not being sustained underground.
- In India, since ancient times dams and canals were used for irrigation. These were made and managed by local people and met the basic requirements of agriculture and daily needs throughout the year.
- After the British came, they made large dams and long distance canals. These mega projects were also followed by government in independent India. These led to the loss of control, over local water sources, by the local people.

Dams

- Dams are made to store water and generate electricity. The stored water is sent to various places through canals, for agricultural purposes. For example, the Indira Gandhi Canal took water to large area of Rajasthan.
- Building of dams displaces people from its site. Also due to mismanagement of water, people close to the source of water grow crops like sugarcane and rice whereas people farther downstream do not get any water.
- Making large dams causes following problems:
  - **Social problems** as many peasants and local tribals are displaced without adequate rehabilitation.
  - **Economic problems** as these are very expensive projects.
  - **Environmental problems** as they result in deforestation and disturb the local habitat.

Due to these reasons various movements have come up against dam construction, e.g., Narmada Bachao Andolan.

Water harvesting

- Watershed management involves soil and water conservation in a scientific manner to increase the biomass production. Its aim is to develop primary resources like land and water, to produce secondary resources like plants and animals without disturbing ecological balance.
- It increases income of the watershed community and also reduces droughts and floods.
- It also increases life of dams and reservoirs.
- Various organizations have been working to revive ancient system of water harvesting as alternatives to the mega projects like dams.
- They have used various techniques to save water such as: digging small lakes and pits, setting up simple watershed systems, making small earthen dams, setting up roof top water collecting units.
  - With these efforts the ground water levels are replenished and rivers are back to life.
- Since ancient times water harvesting is done in India. *Khadins*, tanks and *nadis* in Rajasthan, *bandharas* and *tals* in Maharashtra, *bundhis* in M.P. and U.P., *ahars* and *pynes* in Bihar, and

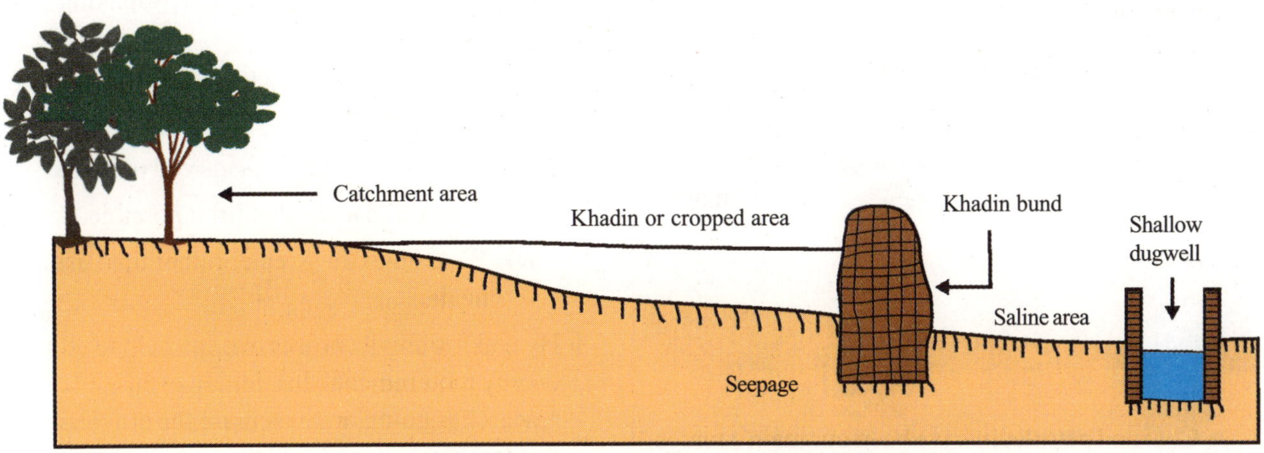

Traditional water harvesting system—Khadin

eris (tanks) in Tamil Nadu, *surangams* in Kerela, *kattas* in Karnataka are ancient ways of storing rain water and are used till date.

- These techniques are local and local people should be allowed to manage these so that mismanagement and over exploitation of the resource is prevented.
- In level terrain, water harvesting structures are crescent shaped earthen embankments or low, straight concrete and rubble 'check dams' built across seasonally flooded gullies.
  - Ponds behind these structures get filled during monsoons. However, only the larger structures hold water year long. Most dry up within six months after monsoons.
  - Their main purpose is not to hold surface water but to replenish ground water. The advantages of ground water are as follows:

    Ground water

    i) does not evaporate
    ii) replenishes wells
    iii) provides water to vegetation
    iv) does not provide ground for mosquito breeding
    v) does not easily get contaminated by human and animal waste.

Questions

1. What is watershed management? (1 mark)
2. Why are dams built? (1 mark)
3. How does the water of the Ganges gets polluted? (2 marks)

Coal and petroleum

- Coal and petroleum have been our main sources of energy since the industrial revolution. With the development of new gadgets and goods to make our lives more convenient, the demand for these energy sources has been increasing exponentially. These resources are not renewable.
- Coal and petroleum were formed by the degradation of biomass millions of years ago. These sources will exhaust in future. According to a study, petroleum will last for about 40 more years and coal for about 200 years. So we need to use these very judiciously. However, there is another problem of pollution related to consumption of coal and petroleum.
- Coal and petroleum contain mainly carbon and hydrogen along with small amounts of nitrogen and sulphur. When these are burnt, oxides of carbon, nitrogen and sulphur are released along with water.
  - Nitrogen oxides and sulphur oxides are toxic and cause acid rain where as carbon dioxide, which is the main product of burning fuel, is a greenhouse gas.
  - Large amounts of carbon dioxide released into air has already led to onset of global warming.
  - Sometimes in the presence of insufficient amount of oxygen, burning coal produces carbon monoxide which is a poisonous gas.
  - However we can make a difference and reduce our energy consumption by making some efforts.

    i) Take a bus or ride a bicycle rather than driving a car.
    ii) Use fluorescent tubes instead of bulbs.
    iii) Take stairs instead of lift if possible.
    iv) Wear an extra sweater rather than using a heater.
- By making small choices, we can help to reduce energy requirements. In addition to this, lot of research is going on to increase the efficiency of our machines to produce maximum energy with minimum air pollution.

EXERCISES

I. Very Short Answer Questions

(1 mark)

1. Which project was launched to improve the quality of Ganga water?
2. What are the three R's to save environment?
3. What is a *Surangam*?
4. What is meant by biodiversity?
5. Name two types of people who benefit from forests.
6. What is bamboo shoot used for?
7. Define sustainable management.
8. Why are coal and petroleum not renewable?
9. What is meant by rain water harvesting?
10. From where did 'Chipko Andolan' start?

II. Short Answer Questions

(2 marks)

1. List different products that can be obtained from forests.
2. How can you assess the quality of drinking water with the help of a pH paper?
3. How are people living near forests dependent on the forests?
4. How do industrialists exploit the forests?
5. Explain how the involvement of local people helped in recovery of *Sal* forests in West Bengal.
6. What are the damages caused to forests by the following?
   a. building tourists spots
   b. Grazing domestic animals
   c. Littering due to tourists' stay and the activities involved in making arrangements for their convenience
7. What are the disadvantages of building dams?
8. How was water harvesting done in different parts of India in older times?
9. What are the disadvantages of burning coal and petroleum?
10. What was the canal system of irrigation followed in ancient India?

III. Short Answer Questions

(3 marks)

1. What is meant by equitable distribution of resources? What forces will be working against it?
2. Explain the three R's of conservation.
3. When and how the local people were excluded from the management of forests and wildlife?
4. What is meant by monoculture? What are its disadvantages?
5. What is meant by watershed management? What is the advantage of watershed management?
6. How were coal and petroleum formed? Why should we use them judiciously?

7. List a few things you can do to reduce the consumption of energy/fuel.
8. Why do we need to conserve forests? Suggest a few ways in which this can be done.
9. How does Ganges get polluted by human interference? Give three points.
10. Explain a water harvesting structure. What are its advantages over open lakes and reservoirs?
11. 'Replenishment of forests is essential.' Justify the statement by giving any three reasons.
12. Suggest three ways to maintain a balance between environment and development.
13. Write a short note on conservation of forests.

IV. Long Answer Questions

(5 marks)

1. Explain the traditional water harvesting system with a suitable diagram.
2. Explain the role of forests in conserving the environment. How do the forest get depleted? What are its consequences?

TEST YOURSELF

Multiple-Choice Questions

Choose the correct option.

1. Which among the following is not a fossil fuel?
   (a) petroleum (b) coal
   (c) CNG (d) oxygen
2. When did Amrita Devi Bishnoi and many other people sacrificed their lives to save trees?
   (a) 1731 (b) 1931
   (c) 1982 (d) 1795
3. Which among the following is a greenhouse gas?
   (a) carbon dioxide (b) sulphur dioxide
   (c) nitrogen dioxide (d) carbon monoxide
4. Water harvesting is a method which
   (a) increases the level of ground water
   (b) decreases the level of ground water
   (c) leads to run-off water
   (d) leads to purification of water
5. Building of a dam leads to?
   (a) generation of electricity
   (b) irrigation
   (c) control flooding which either stops or slows the amount of water in the river
   (d) all the above

Answers to Multiple-Choice Questions

1. (d) 2. (a) 3. (a)
4. (a) 5. (d)